10, 27, 33, 39, 46, 49, 50, 52, 54
116, 117–118,

FRAGILE COALITIONS: THE POLITICS OF ECONOMIC ADJUSTMENT

Joan M. Nelson and contributors:

John Waterbury
Stephan Haggard
Robert R. Kaufman
Laurence Whitehead
Joan M. Nelson
Thomas M. Callaghy
Miles Kahler

Series Editors:
Valeriana Kallab
Richard E. Feinberg

Transaction Books
New Brunswick (USA) and Oxford (UK)

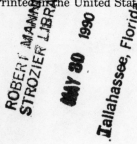

Fragile Coalitions: The Politics of Economic Adjustment

Acknowledgments

Guest Editor:
Joan M. Nelson

Series Editors:
Valeriana Kallab
Richard E. Feinberg

The Overseas Development Council gratefully acknowledges the support of The Ford Foundation, The Rockefeller Foundation, and The William and Flora Hewlett Foundation for the Council's overall program, and of The Pew Charitable Trusts for the ODC U.S.-Third World Policy Perspectives series, of which this policy study is part. Additional funding for this particular volume was provided by The Ford Foundation and The Rockefeller Foundation through their support of ODC's research project on the politics of adjustment.

On behalf of the Council and the contributing authors, the editors wish to express special thanks to participants in the workshop at which early versions of the chapters were discussed.

The editors wish to acknowledge the contributions of Melissa Vaughn, Patricia A. Masters, and Danielle Currier to the editorial preparation of this book, and to Joycelyn Critchlow for processing of the manuscript.

Contents

Overview

The Politics of Long-Haul Economic Reform

Joan M. Nelson

As the 1990s approach, the assumptions and mindsets that have guided economic policies for the past quarter-century in most of Africa, since the late 1940s in China and India, for as long or longer in much of Latin America, and for seventy years in the Soviet Union are being challenged and significantly revamped. These changes involve complex technical economic problems. They also entail bitter and intense political conflicts.

This volume focuses on the political dimensions of economic reform, particularly in Latin America and Africa. In these two regions, and in some other developing nations as well, economic reorientation in the 1980s has been paradoxically both spurred and hobbled by the hostile international economic climate and the debt overhang. International changes have spotlighted the costs of earlier national economic policies, reinforcing arguments for new strategies. But mounting debt burdens and adverse terms of trade have also meant chronic fiscal and balance-of-payments crises, making austerity the backdrop of longer-term reform efforts. Opposition to austerity has merged with and heightened political conflict over economic liberalization—that is, steps toward a more limited state role in the economy and a more open stance toward international economic transactions.

In the course of the 1980s, the prevailing assumptions regarding the nature of the economic crisis gripping much of Africa and Latin America have changed, as have assessments of the duration and scope of measures needed to restart sustainable growth. Initial approaches were dominated by "quick-fix" assumptions, sketched in the first section of

3

this overview. By the decade's end, however, it is clear that for most developing nations, economic reorientation is a long-haul proposition, as outlined in the second section. The political obstacles to long-haul reform are explored next, followed by consideration of how such reform interacts with other goals—including poverty alleviation and consolidation of new or restored democracy. The chapter closes with a discussion of the implications of the politics of long-haul economic reform for external agencies and creditor nations. Many of the key points signaled in this overview are more fully explored in the chapters that follow.

Early 1980s: The "Quick-Fix" Scenario

When the debt crisis broke, and for some time thereafter, the prevailing view in international financial and development circles was that while prompt and vigorous action by both creditors and debtors was imperative, appropriate corrective actions could fairly rapidly restore balance and permit resumed growth. This in turn would permit the resumption of "normal" international financial relations, including debt service and fresh capital inflows. The debtor nations needed sharp but presumably temporary curtailment of demand and adjustment of severely distorted prices, including exchange and interest rates and producer and consumer subsidies. Proponents of this view expected that the "fix" would be painful but quick—a matter of a few years at most.

This quick-fix scenario, it must be readily conceded, applied much more to Latin America than to Africa; and within Latin America it applied more to certain countries than to others. It was also widely recognized that in addition to the stabilization and correction of price distortions, sustainable growth would usually require medium-term, supply-side changes—altered patterns of investment and more efficient production. Precisely to encourage these medium-term reforms, the World Bank in 1980 introduced Structural Adjustment Loans (SALs), later supplemented by Sector Adjustment Loans (SECALs). But even the "medium term" was fairly brief: The Bank initially assumed that structural adjustment lending to a country would continue for three to five years. And understandably, short-run issues of international financial stability dominated the agenda, and quick-fix assumptions influenced the expectations of most other international players—the major creditor governments, the International Monetary Fund (IMF), and the commercial banks—as well as those of hard-pressed debtor governments.

The quick-fix approach carried clear implications for the political challenges within debtor nations. The politics of adjustment was viewed as mainly a matter of overcoming obstacles to needed measures, particularly the risk of mass urban protest against austerity measures. External agencies often assumed that the vital precondition was sufficient political will on the part of national leaders to "bite the bullet" and ensure that the policies were adopted. Most of the measures needed were of the kind that could be set in motion by central economic agencies: ministries of finance and central banks.

The key political problem, according to this scenario, was that benefits lagged behind costs. Costs were obvious and immediate, while benefits were delayed; many of those who stood to gain doubted that the benefits would materialize, or that they would in fact reach them. The timing of adjustment packages and the phasing of specific measures in principle might be designed to try to minimize opposition, but in practice the urgency of the crisis left little room for choosing opportune moments, and the relatively short time frame (and the technical need for certain measures to be implemented simultaneously) limited the possibilities for phasing. The logic of the quick-fix scenario therefore focused attention on tactics that might reduce opposition: persuasion, partial compensation, obfuscation, and subtle or not-so-subtle threats. If the economy (and the foreign commercial banks) responded as expected to adjustment efforts, the results would benefit almost everyone and would soon pacify most opponents. Economic recovery would also facilitate the implementation of necessary medium-term supply-side reforms. Opposition would be narrower and easier to manage, and growth itself would facilitate partial compensation to reduce opposition from groups suffering long-term losses.

The Shift to Long-Haul Perceptions

By the latter half of the 1980s, both developing countries and international financial and development circles were substantially revising their assumptions. Many developing countries clearly were in deeper economic difficulties than they, and often the external agencies, had initially recognized. Distortions and disincentives for productive investment were more pervasive, institutional weaknesses more widespread and fundamental, and supply responses often slower and weaker than anticipated. External agencies were increasingly convinced that, in addition to better macroeconomic management and price reforms, far-reaching institutional changes, restructured public investment patterns, and revised development strategies were essential to restart growth on a sustainable basis.

Domestic and foreign business confidence proved much harder to restore than the quick-fix scenario had anticipated. In part, investors' skepticism often reflected adverse international economic trends. Moreover, stabilization and adjustment measures sometimes conflicted: New export incentives, for instance, were sometimes rendered moot by the scarcity of credit and foreign exchange. But the very credibility of government policies and programs was also often shaky. Many in the business community opposed some of the changes, but both supporters and opponents were often skeptical that fragile stabilization and specific investment incentives would endure. Price changes, in particular, were subject both to erosion (through inflation and real exchange rate appreciation) and to administrative reversal. Put differently, the same features that make price reforms comparatively easy to implement may also make them unconvincing to investors. The impact of all of these factors has been capital flight and low investment in most countries. In the poorest nations, private sector firms and markets are also inherently weak; even where they have responded to favorable policies, they build from extremely low bases.

Moreover, international economic trends and the commercial banks did not perform as initially expected. With some exceptions, non-oil commodity terms of trade continued their long-term decline. The industrialized nations recovered from the sharp depression of 1980–82 but did not regain the growth rates of earlier decades, which dampened demand for products from developing countries. Protection increased in the advanced nations—particularly against exports from the newly industrialized countries (NICs). Agricultural subsidies in rich nations may have had still more pernicious effects on the exports of many developing countries. Early assumptions that foreign commercial banks would respond to improved economic policies in developing countries also proved false. In many countries, inadequate or negative net resource flows crippled recovery efforts. While some relief looks probable as the decade closes, the various approaches being considered do not promise major reversals—positive net flows—for most of the heavily indebted countries.

For all of these reasons, economic adjustment and sustainable growth now appear to require far broader reforms, over a much longer period of time, than the quick-fix scenario envisaged. The prospect of a long haul has major implications for the politics of adjustment.

The Politics of Long-Haul Economic Adjustment

The politics of long-haul adjustment reflects the hostile international economic trends, the intertwining of austerity and economic liberalization, and the unexpectedly complex problems of liberalization itself.

The External Setting and Basic Attitudes Toward Reform

The East Asian "tigers"—Taiwan, Korea, Singapore, and Hong Kong—restructured their distorted economies in the 1960s in an international setting that was conducive to growth. In these countries, the psychological and political results were an environment of hope and the perception that their own choices and actions would largely determine their national economic prospects. In the 1980s, in contrast, governments, organized interests, and the general public in nations being urged to adopt difficult reforms are well aware of the hostile international setting. Virtually everywhere the growing burden of debt has aroused bitter anger, well captured in former Tanzanian President Julius Nyerere's agonized query, "Must we starve our children to pay our debts?" Especially in smaller and poorer countries, the long decline in the prices of many commodity exports, protectionism in the industrial world, and intense competition from the dynamic NICs also evoke despair and the widespread feeling that sacrifices and reforms are likely to be futile.

Austerity and Adjustment Fatigue

In addition to the anger and pessimism prompted by the international setting, the combination of prolonged austerity and economic liberalization has generated much more sustained internal political conflict than anticipated in the quick-fix scenario.

Short-run austerity measures such as wage freezes or reduced food or fuel subsidies often catalyze mass protests, which make global headlines. But a determined government can usually contain or ride out such protests and continue its program; Venezuela in March 1989 is a recent example, among many others. Moreover, if there is a widely perceived crisis and the government can present its program as a plausible solution, many people and groups may be willing to undergo short-run sacrifices for their own benefit and that of the country as a whole.

But continued acquiescence depends on demonstrated results. The general public and even the educated elite in most countries mainly judge the government's economic management by their own economic situations. They cannot be expected to consider whether things would be still worse in the absence of the policies adopted, nor to separate the tangled interactions of announced policies, actual government actions (which may depart considerably from announcements), and factors beyond government control (such as weather or trends in international markets). In many countries, continued economic stagnation or decay has destroyed popular confidence in the government's ability to manage the economy, as well as confirmed initial skepticism about the effects of the policies urged by external agencies.

The efficacy of the tactics employed to manage opposition that were mentioned earlier—persuasion, partial compensation, obfuscation, and containment—rapidly depreciates in the absence of tangible improvements. In Latin America as the decade ends, adjustment fatigue is reflected in rising support for "populist" electoral candidates promising relief for "the little man," as demonstrated in the victories of Michael Manley in Jamaica, Carlos Andres Perez in Venezuela, and Carlos Menem in Argentina; the unexpectedly strong showing of Cuauhtemoc Cárdenas in Mexico; and the distinct probability of a "populist" victory in the upcoming elections in Brazil. Such victories may or may not presage irresponsible economic policies (there are no such signs in Venezuela or Jamaica), but they do signal altered coalitions of support and pressures on governments.

Economic Liberalization and Established Interests

Not only the lengthened timetable, but the broadened reform agenda intensifies the political challenge. Structural reforms intended to liberalize the economy pose different threats to established interests than do stabilization packages. Demand restraint is ostensibly temporary, even though "temporary" seems to be stretching out indefinitely in many cases. But economic liberalization entails a wide array of permanent measures that threaten many groups with severe long-term losses. Among the most obvious: More open trade puts at risk all but the most efficient of the manufacturing firms that grew up behind high protective walls. A diminished role for the state threatens not only the jobs of public sector workers but also the hopes for employment of many of the young people graduating from college or even from secondary school. In Costa Rica, for example, the public sector employed a fifth of all workers by 1980; two out of every five new jobs were public sector jobs; and a still higher proportion of educated youth looked to the government as their prospective employer.[1] In some African countries, the public sector employs as many as half of all wage workers. For these groups—among the most politically potent—no apparent later benefits can serve to balance immediate and severe losses.

In contrast, many of the beneficiaries of adjustment measures are unorganized, as is often the case with rural smallholders. In Ghana, for instance, cocoa and other export cultivators have probably gained from sharply increased producer prices and dramatic devaluation, but the government has yet to mobilize and channel their political support without at the same time activating simmering urban discontent.[2] There is no one-to-one correlation between economic gains and political support; much depends on how the gainers fit into existing political institutions and processes.[3] Moreover, some potential gainers have not yet actually benefited, including the entrepreneurs who may emerge to take advantage of new incentives and opportunities; they can hardly be expected to constitute a counterweight to opponents of reform. And in some Sub-Saharan African countries, the impression is widespread that the main winners from liberalization are foreigners—the resident non-African commercial, financial, and small manufacturing community

(Asians in East Africa, "Lebanese" in parts of West Africa); multinational corporations; and the influx of expatriate advisors. In this view, structural adjustment threatens one of the main pillars of post-independence politics: the assertion of indigenous African control of the economy.

Administrative Features of Economic Liberalization

The politics of the long haul also reflects administrative contrasts between most structural changes (other than price adjustments) and the macroeconomic and price reform agenda of the quick-fix scenario. Most instruments of short-run stabilization, including fiscal austerity, credit ceilings, interest rate adjustments, and devaluation, are largely or wholly within the control of central economic authorities. Many can be decreed by the stroke of a pen—though implementing and maintaining the adjustments may require more complex moves. In contrast, many structural adjustment measures are not entirely or even largely within the control of central economic authorities. Often they require legislative approval. To be carried out, measures like trade liberalization or state enterprise reform demand cooperation from a number of governmental agencies (and sometimes private groups), whose directors and staffs often do not understand and/or fundamentally oppose the changes. Thus there are any number of openings for accidental or deliberate sabotage. Moreover, because the process is protracted, ample opportunities exist for those who stand to lose, inside and outside the government, to organize themselves and to form coalitions to oppose change.

Limiting the Role of the State and the "Orthodox Paradox"

The anti-state nature of many of the reforms urged by external agencies further deepens the difficulties. Governments must rely on their officials to carry out reforms. Officials with a genuine commitment to their agencies and programs often deeply resent what they view as external attacks. More broadly, measures to streamline or privatize public enterprises, to tighten central economic agencies' control over budgets and expenditures, and to eliminate a wide variety of state controls and regulations over economic activity and convert others (import licensing, allocation of credit) from criteria within the discretion of state officers to quasi-automatic criteria or mechanisms all constitute a direct assault on the interests of many public employees. Such reforms put jobs at risk, as well as diminish opportunities for side payments. When thousands of workers are laid off, even those still on the payroll wonder who will be next. Less obviously, especially in Africa, higher-level public employees may hold extensive interests in private enterprises that benefit from existing regulations. These holdings may be fully legal, but they none-theless constitute a major conflict of interest.

At the highest levels, political leaders have vested political (as dis-tinct from economic) interests in retaining discretion over the allocation of resources such as foreign exchange, bank credit, import licenses, and jobs. Such discretion may facilitate corruption, but in many countries it is also the main instrument for building and maintaining support coali-tions. Even where top leaders are persuaded that reforms are impera-tive, they may not be able to follow through if the public sector itself constitutes a major component of their political support. This was the fatal weakness of Zambian President Kenneth Kaunda's reform effort, which collapsed in mid-1987. In Miles Kahler's telling phrase, the "orthodox paradox" is the attempt to use the agencies and personnel of the state to diminish or dismantle their own power.

The Need for a More Effective State Capacity

There is a deeper level of the "orthodox paradox." Neoclassical advo-cates argue that economic liberalization requires a diminished, less interventionist state, but it has become increasingly evident that resumed and sustainable growth also requires increased state capabili-ties—not so much a less powerful state as one that plays different roles and does so more effectively. Historically, in the now industrialized nations, economic growth went hand in hand with an increased state capacity to maintain law and order and provide expanding infrastruc-ture and public services, including education. This required not only improved organization and technical abilities, but the development of a public service ethic. Until well into the nineteenth century, public office in many now industrialized nations was either purchased or bestowed as a political or personal reward. Officials high and low viewed their positions not as a public trust but as an investment to be recovered, or a personal privilege to be exploited. As Thomas Callaghy suggests in his chapter in this volume, the slow evolution of a genuine civil service was linked to larger changes in systems of political support and control. Colonial bureaucracies were shielded from nationalistic politics; after independence, the linking of bureaucracy to politics often meant reduced efficiency. This perspective sheds light on the decline, in many African countries over the past two decades, of state capacity to perform even such routine functions as road repairs.

The argument is not that all reforms must be in place before any can take effect, nor that fundamental problems of state building must be resolved before economic adjustment can begin. Many structural changes can be made within relatively short periods, and many others within a decade or two. But weaknesses of the larger administrative set-ting will frequently hamper reforms and constrain their effects.

Callaghy has these limits in mind when he warns against inflated hopes for "institution building" and argues (with Kenneth Waltz) that necessities do not create possibilities. The more thoroughgoing reform of the state, he points out, will mirror—indeed will be an integral part of—longer-term political and social conflict and change.

Political Constraints and the Record to Date

The track record of adjustment efforts during the 1980s reflects these internal political obstacles, though any appraisal must also take into account the effects of adverse external trends. One way to assess the record is to ask which sectors or types of reforms have fared best and worst, as gauged by implementation efforts (not by economic outcomes). Based on the experience of fifteen countries where adjustment measures have been in place for some years, the World Bank's most recent appraisal concludes that exchange rates and pricing policies in general have shown the greatest change. Pricing policies, as noted earlier, are precisely those that are administratively easiest to alter. As the same logic leads us to expect, progress has been far slower with institutional and non-price reforms, and with those aspects of pricing policies that require institutional changes to remain effective. Import liberalization, tax reform, and the reform of state economic enterprises (including divestiture) have all proved politically contentious and administratively complex. Many governments have cut the losses of state enterprise by reducing subsidies or increasing the prices of their products, but more complex administrative reforms have lagged.

Fiscal deficits narrowed in many countries for several years in the early and mid-1980s, but have tended to widen recently—especially in Sub-Saharan Africa and other heavily indebted countries elsewhere—reflecting the debt burden and rising domestic political pressures. Perhaps most disturbing for future prospects, investment relative to gross domestic product (GDP) has dwindled sharply in many countries, reflecting both brutal public sector cuts and the private sector loss of confidence discussed earlier. Only in a handful of countries has investment begun to recover.[4]

A brief overview of the political factors common to almost all of the countries adopting and implementing vigorous economic adjustment programs offers additional evidence regarding the politics of adjustment. Among those governments pursuing particularly far-reaching programs of economic reorientation in the 1980s (plus a few cases from the 1970s), most share important political features. Consider Chile after 1973, Sri Lanka from 1977 to the early 1980s, Turkey and Jamaica since 1980, Ghana since 1983, and the Philippines since 1986. SUCCESS STORIES All of these countries had suffered long periods—in Ghana's case, two decades—of economic stagnation or decline or of deepening financial crisis, coupled with increasingly widespread political alienation and/or polarization and violence. In each, in the years noted (in Ghana, at the very end of 1981), a new government took office, elected with overwhelming majorities in Sri Lanka, Jamaica, and the Philippines; and taking power in military coups but with considerable or sweeping public support in Chile, Turkey, and Ghana. In all of these countries, there was clearly widespread support—indeed *demand*—for major changes, although there were deep divisions in every case regarding the nature of the needed reforms. In Sri Lanka and Jamaica, the new heads of state held firm views on the direction of reform; not coincidentally, both hoped to avoid austerity and rely on expansionary adjustments. In the other cases, internal and (especially in Ghana) external advisors shaped the programs adopted, but commitment to change was a shared feature.

Despite their varying political systems, moreover, all six governments had highly centralized authority. In Chile, Turkey (between 1980 and 1983), and Ghana, military rule ensured control. While Philippine President Corazon Aquino had come to power on a wave of popular support, she ruled by executive decree during her first eighteen months in office. In Sri Lanka and Jamaica, both long-established parliamentary democracies, Prime Ministers Julius Jayawardene and Edward Seaga both were powerful leaders who thoroughly dominated their cabinets, parties, and legislatures. (Both also tightened their control after several years in office by maneuvers widely viewed as erosions of democratic tradition.) In all six cases, moreover, organized opposition groups were routed and in disarray for the first years of the new governments; in the military cases they were also suppressed.

In short, all of these cases shared a *reform syndrome:* Leaders firmly committed to major change, widespread public acceptance or demand for such change, new governments with strong centralized authority, and a disabled opposition constituted the political context for determined adjustment efforts.[5]

Another outstanding example of a strong adjustment program fits the reform syndrome somewhat less fully. In Mexico, the years before the crisis of 1982 were not a period of economic stagnation and political decay; nor was there corresponding public demand for change. But important segments of the ruling elite felt that the economic and political trends of roughly the previous decade were unsustainable. Once the debt crisis had erupted, the formidable institutional control of the established dominant party and its blend of co-option and suppression of dissenting groups, such as the major labor unions, permitted the draconian adjustment efforts of the de la Madrid government. Narrower public consensus was compensated for by greater central power.

A glance at Argentina is also instructive. When Raúl Alfonsín took office, Argentina shared most of the features of the reform syndrome described above: protracted economic stagnation, political alienation and polarization (hence a widespread demand for fundamental change), a new government elected with a strong majority, and elements of the opposition (clearly the military and less clearly the Peronist unions) in disarray. And indeed the Austral Plan, coupled with more orthodox macroeconomic measures, slowed inflation for several years and seemed to offer a setting for longer-term structural changes. But reforms stalled as the nation's traditionally formidable interest groups regained their footing. By then, Alfonsín's power was not great enough to cope with revived opposition.

Other countries have adopted piecemeal reforms, but lack some elements of the reform syndrome. In many countries, commitment to reform has never extended beyond a small circle of technocrats with at best tentative and temporary backing from political leaders. And many governments are too fragile and their span of control too limited to adopt and implement structural reforms—even if they have managed to pursue short-term austerity programs for a year or two.

Tactics, Phasing, and Compromise

As John Waterbury discusses in detail in another chapter in this volume, even where political leaders are committed to change and have considerable power, tactics, and strategy can make the difference between effective and failed reform efforts. Laurence Whitehead and Thomas Callaghy join Waterbury in arguing that compensatory payments to the most politically potent losers are often essential, even where such payments conflict with equity considerations and with economic efficiency in a narrow sense. Shrewd phasing is perhaps a still more important element of coalition management. The key is to avoid alienating too many groups at once and to keep potential opposition groups isolated from each other.   *see:* Hassaro 1993

Phased reforms also ease problems of leadership and management. The implementation of virtually all significant reforms requires sustained top-level attention. Even changes in key prices (including devaluation) demand supporting measures and follow-up actions to avoid erosion. But no leader, however committed, can give adequate attention to more than a short list of adjustment issues at any one time. Both coalition management and the span of control therefore argue for careful phasing. Of course technicians cannot freely mix and match policies to ease political and administrative problems; some measures have to be implemented at the same time. But economic considerations may also counsel phasing. For example, tariff reduction undertaken as part of import liberalization can worsen fiscal problems. Recent reappraisals of East Asian success stories emphasize the phased nature of the reforms:

initial vigorous export expansion—followed only considerably later (and with great reluctance) by some import liberalization.[6] It is worth considering the merits, in specific country circumstances, of "Fabian strategy and blitzkrieg tactics" for adjustment—isolating sets of issues from each other, but handling each set rapidly and firmly before opposition can mobilize.[7]

Beyond or in addition to phasing and other techniques for coalition management, shifts from state-led to more market-oriented approaches, and from import-substituting to more open trade regimes, will predictably generate conflicts that must be resolved through compromise. Even the most ardently free-trade industrialized states balanced the opening of their economies with measures to shield domestic business and labor interests from the full impact of foreign competition. In the smaller Western European democracies, heavy dependence on international trade has been combined with unusual political stability and social welfare by precisely such blends of sustained liberal trade policies coupled with extensive buffering mechanisms and measures.[8] Put differently, long-haul economic liberalization must be pursued jointly with other goals, and it entails compromises to accommodate those goals.

Balancing Economic Adjustment and Other Goals

Returning to the quick-fix notion, it is roughly accurate to argue that in the early 1980s the international financial and development agencies pressed debtor governments to subordinate virtually all other goals to stabilization and adjustment. The economic crisis also crowded out other issues from the domestic agenda of most debtors. The specter of international financial collapse and the limits of financing left little room for manuever, while the expected rapid economic turnaround seemed to justify temporarily sidelining other goals. In most cases little attention was paid to distributive effects—in part because the data needed to support useful analysis were not available, but also because both international agencies and their allies within developing-country governments were convinced that economic recovery was the most powerful means to ease the deprivations of depression, and that recovery was "just around the corner"—or at worst a bit further down the road. Possible threats to the consolidation of democracy resulting from adjustment measures were not a focus of attention for a different reason: Although several smaller nations had moved in democratic directions earlier, the wave of democratic transitions was not obvious until 1984, when Brazil, Argentina, and Turkey all elected new governments. In some countries, even the claims of national security were temporarily subordinated as military budgets were contained or even cut more than proportionately to other expenditures.

But as the time horizon lengthened, competing concerns—such as the government's longer-term political prospects, pressures for political reform, national security and prestige, poverty alleviation—could no longer be postponed, either by governments or by external actors. An obvious illustration is the wave of international concern and action in the late 1980s to buffer the poor and vulnerable from the effects of economic depression and adjustment measures. Equally clear is the growing anxiety about tensions between adjustment and continued transition to democracy in many countries. And pressure is increasing, mainly from Northern governments and groups, for increased attention to protecting the environment in the course of adjustment and renewed growth.

Not only the longer time horizon but also the broadened economic reform agenda makes it increasingly difficult to view economic adjustment in isolation from other goals. It is useful to distinguish here between macroeconomic austerity measures and structural reforms to liberalize the economy. Even though measures to contain rampant inflation and ballooning fiscal and balance-of-payments deficits can prompt intense conflicts over who bears the costs, the goals themselves are widely viewed as desirable, indeed essential. And there is substantial technical consensus on the kinds of measures that must be taken. But when the agenda broadens to include structural changes and medium-term development strategies, different views regarding goals, values, and priorities become salient and technical consensus wanes.[9] Many economists have doubts about how fast and far export promotion and import liberalization should be pushed in particular countries, nor can small countries' concerns about food security or broader vulnerability to international shocks be lightly dismissed. And despite the new global consensus that extensive central planning works badly, there is room for wide variation in views and practice regarding the appropriate role of the state in the economy. Different resolutions of these issues will not only determine the speed and effectiveness of economic recovery and adjustment, but also powerfully affect other goals and values.

Democracy and Economic Adjustment

Conventional wisdom has long held that authoritarian governments are more likely than democracies to adopt and enforce unpopular economic stabilization and adjustment measures. They are assumed to be better placed to make long-run plans, less influenced by popular pressures, and better able to both forestall protest through anticipated repression and suppress protest if it does occur. In the longer run, moreover, democracies are perceived to be more likely to develop powerful entrenched interest groups that block flexible adaptation to changing technology or international trends.[10]

Several considerations sharply challenge these assumptions. Authoritarian systems, especially long-established ones, are hardly immune to problems of inflexible vested interests. And as noted earlier, some democracies, such as those in several of the smaller Western European nations, have developed sophisticated channels and procedures to accommodate all major interests while permitting adaptation to changing economic circumstances. Sclerosis is neither unique to, nor endemic among, established democracies. Two recent studies of economic stabilization in large samples of developing countries found no systematic association between regime type and the ability to stabilize. But as already noted, in those democracies that carried through broad economic reforms in the 1980s, opposition groups had been temporarily weakened.[11]

A variant on this issue has come to the fore with the wave of turns or returns to democracy in the 1980s in much of Latin America and in the Philippines, Korea, Taiwan, Pakistan, Turkey, Tunisia, Nigeria, and elsewhere. Many of these countries face the simultaneous challenges of consolidating political liberalization while pursuing difficult economic adjustments.

Two chapters in this volume examine the links between these processes. Stephan Haggard and Robert Kaufman focus on the extent and ways in which transitions to more open political systems affect macroeconomic management. They offer evidence that established democratic governments do not generally have greater difficulties controlling fiscal and monetary policy than do authoritarian regimes, but the new (or renewed) democratic governments do have special problems. Often the economic management troubles of governments in transition to democracy can be traced in part to the economic legacies inherited from authoritarian predecessors. But the process of democratic transition itself also generates pressures. New democracies usually must contend with high levels of political participation and expectations as well as with discontinuities in policymaking authority and institutions. Their own populist strategies may compound their problems. However, some new democracies have launched significant economic reforms, capitalizing on the disarray of the opposition, the ability to blame the costs on the old regime, and sometimes on an unusual concentration of power in the early stages of transition. The Philippines under Aquino is one salient example.

Laurence Whitehead's discussion of disinflation and democratic consolidation is cast in a longer time frame. Whitehead starts from the premise that in Latin America disinflation and consolidation of democracy are both goals of the highest priority. Neither can be subordinated to the other (except briefly) without setting in motion forces likely to ultimately destroy both. Both processes may be set in train by rapid and intense measures or events, but can be consolidated only through a much longer period of building trust—in new arrangements for containing and aligning prices (including wages) throughout the economy and in democratic institutions. Whitehead's arguments might well extend to countries outside Latin America with similar economic problems and high political participation—including the Philippines, Turkey, Tunisia, Nigeria, and Pakistan.

Economic Adjustment, Equity, and Poverty Alleviation

My own essay (Chapter 4) turns to the links between adjustment and another urgent goal: poverty alleviation. As already noted, international efforts of the 1970s to address basic human needs and to encourage redistribution with growth were subordinated in the early 1980s, but they reemerged with added urgency as the social costs of depression and adjustment became painfully evident later in the decade. The chapter focuses on the political issues of pursuing "adjustment with a human face," starting with the fact that protecting the poor—pressed more vigorously by outside agencies than by domestic forces—is usually a fairly low-priority objective for political leaders.

As UNICEF's well-known study argues, in most countries there is scope for measures to protect some of the poor and to improve their long-term access to productive resources and health and education services despite the constraints of austerity.[12] But with the exception of short-term externally financed relief, most pro-poor measures entail shifting resources from better off groups, including lower-middle and near-poor classes. Such measures inevitably generate strong political resistance. Moreover, these same middle-class and near-poor groups, particularly in the cities, often have been hard hit by depression and adjustment. They are not the most vulnerable, but they may be the most aggrieved victims of the decade's lost growth. Compensatory programs often do help these groups. In contrast, the tightly targeted pro-poor measures also advocated by international agencies and Northern governments are not likely to soothe growing adjustment fatigue and political resistance.

In short, the "equity issue" as perceived in developing countries is not the same as the "poverty issue" of greatest concern in international circles. The strategies most likely to prove politically sustainable may be those that reorient services and investments to benefit both some among the poor and some among the more politically potent middle deciles.

External Agencies and the Politics of Long-Term Adjustment

How do these varied political implications of long-haul adjustment bear on the role and tactics of external agencies?

The coalition of major creditor governments, the IMF, the World Bank, and the commercial banks has played a central role in the design of stabilization and liberalization efforts in the 1980s. There are some major exceptions. In some countries, including the largest, the impetus for economic restructuring has been almost wholly internal. Turkey, India, China, and the Soviet Union are clear examples. In other cases, acute external crisis in the early 1980s combined with older internal concerns to prompt far-reaching reorientation—as in Mexico and Jamaica. In much of Africa and Latin America, however, restructuring has been almost entirely forced by external events and agencies. Indeed, the 1980s has seen external intervention in internal economic policies to a degree unprecedented in terms of the measures addressed and the number of countries involved.

Conditionality, Finance, and Debt Reduction

Increased use of conditionality has been a major feature of this type of donor intervention. IMF stand-by agreements had always entailed targets and conditions; what was new was the number of countries with such agreements and the frequency of a string of back-to-back stand-bys that stretched programs originally conceived as short-term into semi-permanent arrangements. The scope of IMF conditions also was considerably broadened in arrangements under the Extended Fund Facility (EFF) and the more recent Structural Adjustment Facility (SAF) and Enhanced Structural Adjustment Facility (ESAF). Meanwhile, the World Bank shifted a quarter of its loans from the traditional project form into structural and sector loans conditioned on policy reforms.

A decade's experience with expanded conditionality provides some clear lessons about its potential as well as its limits. As noted earlier, conditionality is much more effective at promoting specific, readily monitored measures that can be executed fairly rapidly by central economic authorities—most typically, demand containment and price changes. More complex measures that involve more agencies and groups and entail institutional changes, such as trade liberalization, are harder. SALs and ESAFs promote such reforms less effectively not only because the reforms themselves are more difficult, but because the loans do not provide incentives to all of the key actors involved. Central economic authorities and political leaders are eager—often desperate—for the financing that such loans provide, and therefore reforms within their direct authority are likely to be carried out (at least initially). But the public enterprise pressed to sharply reduce the number of its employees, or the commodity marketing board urged to restructure its prices and procedures, has little to gain from a balance-of-payments loan. Such an agency will comply only to the extent that it lacks the administrative autonomy or political support to resist.[13]

The influence of conditionality varies not only among types of policies but also among countries. Actual compliance is greatest where governments are already strongly committed to reform. As Miles Kahler discusses in Chapter 6, however, external influence—that is, the extent to which external persuasion, support, and pressure cause a government to change its policy trajectory—is likely to be greater where commitment is less strong. But where both commitment and capacity are very weak, conditionality has not proved very effective in promoting more complex medium-term reforms, though conditions can shape short-run macroeconomic measures. Moreover, especially in smaller nations and those with limited administrative capabilities, external agencies' efforts to enforce "agreed-upon" structural reforms often have led to detailed and invasive monitoring of the relevant sectors or policies. Such monitoring has itself become an issue in the internal politics of debtors and an increasing irritant in their relations with external agencies.

There is of course no clear division between governments prepared to undertake significant reforms and those not ready to do so. External agencies' staffs often must gauge whether additional finance coupled with conditions will alter domestic pressures enough to give reform a fighting chance—a subtle and dicey judgment call. But by the late 1980s, it is clear that structural adjustment lending with its complex conditionality has been extended to many more countries than such judgments would warrant. The original thinking behind World Bank SALs envisaged a highly selective process. The broadened application of structural adjustment lending partly reflected the external agencies' conviction that reform is urgent, and that delay simply causes additional pain. These convictions may have been reinforced with undue optimism about external leverage—perhaps a legacy from obsolete quick-fix assumptions. But a second cause of overextended structural adjustment lending, which has been increasingly important in the late 1980s, has been the tacit conversion of SALs and SECALs (as well as more recent IMF SAF and ESAF loans) into the main channel of desperately needed balance-of-payments assistance, as other sources of finance have dried up.

In short, the international financial institutions have come under increasing pressure—from major creditor governments as well as debtor countries—to "move money." That mission is sharply at odds with the requisites of successful broad-gauged conditionality: careful design, patient development of consensus, and the credible threat of withholding funds where performance falls short of commitments. Urgent, high-stakes negotiations provide neither time nor motivation for genuine policy dialogue. Instead, they create strong incentives for what Callaghy calls "ritual dances"—in which hard-pressed governments tell international institutions what they have been instructed to say, and the institutions in turn pretend to believe what they hear. Where a country has geopolitical importance, the process becomes still more of a charade, damaging credibility both within and beyond the country immediately concerned.

The growing use of high-conditionality instruments as the main source of financial relief, coupled with the generally inadequate (often net negative) level of financing, has had a further, subtler but pernicious effect in distorting the international financial institutions' own analyses and estimates of prospects for recovery. Given the limited prospects for net positive financing from all sources, IMF and World Bank staff are under pressure to underestimate the time required for governments to implement reforms and for production to respond to changed incentives. In the Fund's case, this pressure grows partly from the need to project repayment within the time required by its facilities. Bank staff are less affected by this consideration, particularly where International Development Association (IDA) funds are used, but may lean toward optimism to encourage the government and perhaps to promote more financing from bilateral and commercial sources. Overoptimistic projections have led to a high incidence of shortfalls in performance—eroding relations between governments and the international institutions, discrediting the countries' own economic officials, and accentuating the decline of public confidence in governments' economic management.

More generally, in a fair number of countries the attempt to link financing to "high" (more properly, "broad") conditionality or requirements for far-reaching reforms, in the context of continuing stagnation or economic decline, has undermined fragile and contingent confidence in the nature of the prescriptions being urged by external agencies. It has contributed to a corrosive mixture of public cynicism, defeatism, and anger—precisely the opposite of the gradual emergence of economic confidence and political trust that Whitehead identifies as crucial both to economic stabilization and (in the relevant countries) to the consolidation of democracy. The pattern damages the durable interests of all of those involved: the governments and people of debtor nations; the international financial institutions, creditor governments, and the broader international economic and political systems; and even the interests (save in the narrowest and most immediate sense) of creditor commercial banks.

It is time to bring the design and extent of conditionality and associated financial support into closer accord with the varying political capabilities of debtor governments and with their ability to use balance-of-payments support to rekindle sustainable growth. Those instruments carrying the broadest conditionality—most clearly SALs and EFFs—should be used quite selectively to support governments that fairly clearly have both strong commitment and the political capacity for the implementation of an integrated program of structural change. Financial support for such governments should be enhanced by debt reduction, as proposed in the Brady Plan. To bolster and maintain the credibility of the effort, the total package of financing and debt reduction should be large enough to permit perceptible easing of austerity for much of the public.

Governments with less commitment and political capacity should be pressed to maintain responsible macroeconomic management and to pursue a narrower range of reforms, most likely supported by World Bank hybrid and sector loans and IMF stand-by arrangements and SAF and ESAF loans, providing that the latter are not loaded down with unrealistically ambitious conditions. At a minimum, the level of overall financing should be adequate to prevent net negative transfers.

The basic notion of partly de-linking balance-of-payments support and debt relief from broad conditionality underlies several recent proposals for "two-tier conditionality." Former senior IMF official David Finch has recently set forth such a scheme for Latin American debtors, entailing the establishment of two new IMF facilities. Percy Mistry, formerly with the World Bank, also proposes a kind of two-tier conditionality as part of a more comprehensive set of recommendations for debt relief for Africa.[14]

Two-tiered conditionality does not imply softer conditionality. Indeed, it is the existing pattern that erodes the credibility of conditionality by setting often unrealistically ambitious conditions that are then either met in letter but not in broader intent, or modified, or partially waived. Narrower but more realistic conditions for the lower tier of governments with limited commitment and capacity would permit creditors to insist that conditions be genuinely fulfilled. Reserving more demanding conditions for the higher tier of more vigorous and capable reformers would similarly restore the integrity of the process.

Nor does two-tier conditionality destroy incentives for broader structural adjustment when political conditions in individual countries permit, *if and only if* more ambitious conditionality is clearly accompanied by increased financing and/or debt reduction. Therefore, effective two-tier conditionality does imply increased total financial flows to permit more adequate support for governments that are pursuing or have already carried through extensive reforms, without further constricting support for those governments currently only capable of less ambitious programs—responsible short-run macroeconomic management plus scattered structural reforms.

The principle of selective conditionality also raises serious doubts about proposals, mainly pressed by private voluntary organizations and sometimes by legislators in the Northern nations, that conditions attached to SALs or (less likely) IMF agreements be used to pursue important goals *additional* to adjustment, such as poverty alleviation, environmental protection, and democratization. Such goals in general share certain characteristics with complex and controversial structural economic reforms: Without strong commitment and corresponding political and administrative capabilities within the government, specific conditions attached to broad structural adjustment loans are likely to win small and temporary victories at the price of deep resentment and additional complications in the ongoing domestic debates on such issues. This does not mean omitting these goals from the structural adjustment agenda. External agencies can and should encourage and assist debtor governments to analyze the effects of adjustment measures on poverty and the environment. They can and should support more specific and direct action as elements of project, hybrid, or sector adjustment loans, the latter including appropriate conditionality.

Making Policy Dialogue More Effective

More selective use of broad conditionality would both facilitate and increase the priority of policy dialogue. Such dialogue is probably the most important means available for external agents to gradually shift governments and public opinion toward the commitment and consensus necessary for broad structural change. More effective dialogue will require:

- Expanding the circle of those involved in the process;
- Upgrading old channels for dialogue and seeking new ones; and
- Making the exchange more genuinely two-way.

As Kahler notes, the need for high-level political attention to reforms and for second- and third-echelon cooperation within the bureaucracy argues for extending policy dialogue both above and below the level of the economic team and key operating ministers who are typically included. Extending dialogue still further, beyond government circles, raises different questions. External agencies usually should not be directly involved in this broader debate, but they can contribute indirectly. One means, Kahler suggests, might be more open and publicized IMF Article IV consultations. Joint research on key country-specific issues by World Bank or regional development bank staff and local government agencies (perhaps including local university or other private participants) might be another channel. The use of "neutral" outside experts to smoothen the resolution of controversial issues between international agency staff and debtor governments offers a third channel.[15] Strengthened World Bank missions resident in debtor countries could also facilitate fuller policy dialogue by reducing the reliance on inevitably hurried visiting teams.

Kahler also highlights a set of issues that have received much less attention: the changes within the international financial institutions that are prerequisites for more effective policy dialogue. These include some extremely thorny issues. Perhaps least controversial in a highly contentious list is the suggestion that the international financial institutions distance themselves somewhat from the coalition of creditor governments and commercial banks, requiring the tacit acquiescence of the major shareholder governments of the Fund and Bank. That step has been at least half-taken with respect to some countries—and the recent agreement to allow the IMF to disburse in the presence of arrears suggests growing support for this posture.

Equally important, at least with respect to the poorest countries, may be reduced behind-the-scenes tension between the Fund and the Bank. Ironically, the Fund's efforts to play a more growth-oriented role vis-à-vis the poorest countries has resulted in arrangements that may impede dialogue with those countries. Sixty-two low-income countries, including most of Sub-Saharan Africa, are eligible for the Fund's Enhanced Structural Adjustment Fund. To qualify, a government must reach agreement with the Fund and the Bank jointly on a Policy Framework Paper to guide its own program and the external agencies' funding and conditionality. But agreement between the two Bretton Woods agencies on the precise diagnosis and prescription for the country is often difficult. Therefore, once the two agencies have arrived at a delicate consensus, there is little scope for the country to propose revisions. Views differ sharply on whether the problem is best addressed by closer collaboration between the Bank and the Fund or by a return to earlier divisions of responsibility.[16] But fuller dialogue with this large set of ESAF-eligible governments is unlikely without some resolution of the problem.

If policy dialogue is to better serve the goal of increasing government commitment and ownership of adjustment programs, it must also become more genuinely two-way: less an attempt to persuade governments of the merits of specific external recommendations and more a mutual effort to define key problems and devise solutions. This shift in approach is particularly needed with respect to the design, pacing, and sequencing of medium-term structural reforms. As noted earlier, these reforms, in contrast to short-run macroeconomic management issues, enjoy less technical consensus and permit a wider range of feasible options. Moreover, they pose more complex political and administrative issues, which government knowledge and judgment are crucial to resolving.

World Bank (and to a lesser degree IMF) practice is already more flexible and pragmatic than free-market rhetoric in Washington would indicate. Two-way dialogue might be facilitated if rhetoric were brought more closely in line with practice. In some countries, more basic shifts in stance are needed: in Kahler's phrase, a willingness to consider alternative diagnoses and to explore, over an extended period of time, the likely costs and benefits of alternative strategic options. Alternative proposals grow out of concerns and perceptions that are genuine whether or not they are based on technically sound analysis. Despite the considerable costs in time and administrative resources, they must be engaged, not dismissed. Moreover, the last decade's record of both limited influence on reform and often disappointing results counsels more open minds among the creditor coalition.

Support from the United States

The experience of the 1980s strongly indicates that more effective encouragement of economic reforms in Latin America and Africa will demand more financing (including debt reduction), more selective use of broad conditionality (and therefore some separation between broad conditionality and debt relief), and expanded and more genuinely two-way dialogue. All of these require the active backing of the major creditor governments—above all the United States.

Throughout the decade, U.S. policy toward recovery and reform in the developing world has been reactive, seeking mainly to limit damage to creditors and to minimize the political difficulties at home caused by measures taken to cope with international debt and depression. Arguably, the approaches adopted have served these goals reasonably well. But as the 1990s approach, the continuing cautious reactive stance is increasingly inadequate on three counts:

1. The goal of preventing severe damage to commercial banks has largely been accomplished, but a continuation of past policies is not likely to stem the spreading arrears that endanger the remaining private financial interests.

2. The costs of current policies to other goals and values are rising; these costs range from dwindling developing-country markets for U.S. exports to irreversible physical and mental damage to many millions of young children who lack adequate nutrition.

3. Moreover, slow and timid responses may let slip a most unusual moment of opportunity. Despite the cynicism and despair found in many developing countries, the opening statement of this overview holds: We are in the midst of a global rethinking of strategies for sustainable growth. Not by coincidence, we are also in the midst of a wave of political liberalization, actual and demanded. Despite the broad reach of these trends, within each individual country they are strongly contested, fragile, usually gradual, and may well be reversed. The outcomes will be largely determined by forces internal to each country. But the actions taken by external agencies can help or hinder the long process of reform. The times call for vision and flexibility—including a much more subtle recognition of the political dynamics of long-haul economic and political liberalization.

Notes

[1] Claudio Gonzalez-Vega, "Fear of Adjusting: The Social Costs of Economic Policies in Costa Rica in the 1970s," in Donald E. Schulz and Douglas H. Graham, *Revolution and Counterrevolution in Central America and the Carribbean* (Boulder, Colo.: Westview Press, 1986).

[2] The Ghanaian government's effort to build a new rural support base is discussed in Emmanuel Gyimah-Boadi, "Economic Recovery and Politics in the PNDC's Ghana," Paper prepared for a workshop on the politics of economic adjustment at the Institute of Development Studies, Sussex University, Sussex, England, 31 March–1 April 1989.

[3] For fuller development of this point, see Stephan Haggard and Robert Kaufman, "The Politics of Stabilization and Structural Adjustment," in Jeffrey D. Sachs, ed., *Developing Country Debt and Economic Performance* (Chicago: University of Chicago Press, 1989).

[4] World Bank, *Adjustment Lending: An Evaluation of Ten Years of Experience* (Washington, D.C.: World Bank, 1989); see especially chapters 3 and 4 for a broad survey of policy reforms.

[5] For a fuller discussion of the political factors influencing adjustment choices and implementation, see Joan Nelson, ed., *Economic Crisis and Policy Choice: The Politics of Adjustment in the Third World* (Princeton, N.J.: Princeton University Press, forthcoming 1990).

[6] See, for example, Colin I. Bradford, Jr., "East Asian Models: Myths and Lessons," in John P. Lewis and Valeriana Kallab, eds., *Development Strategies Reconsidered* (New Brunswick, N.J.: Transaction Books in cooperation with the Overseas Development Council, 1986).

[7] The phrase is Samuel Huntington's—used to describe Ataturk's approach to fundamental reforms in Turkey in the 1930s. Samuel P. Huntington, *Political Order in Changing Societies* (New Haven: Yale University Press, 1968), pp. 344–62.

[8] Peter J. Katzenstein, *Small States in World Markets: Industrial Policy in Europe* (Ithaca, N.Y.: Cornell University Press, 1985).

[9] For a fuller discussion of this point, see Gerald K. Helleiner, "Policy-Based Program Lending: A Look at the Bank's New Role," in Richard E. Feinberg and contributors, *Between Two Worlds: The World Bank's Next Decade* (New Brunswick, N.J.: Transaction Books in cooperation with the Overseas Development Council, 1986).

[10] See Mancur Olsen, *The Rise and Decline of Nations* (New Haven, Conn.: Yale University Press, 1982); and Pranab Bardhan, *The Political Economy of Development in India* (Oxford, England: Basil Blackwell, 1984).

[11] Stephan Haggard, "The Politics of Adjustment: Lessons from the IMF's Extended Fund Facility," in Miles Kahler, ed., *The Politics of International Debt* (Ithaca, N.Y.: Cornell University Press, 1986); Karen Remmer, "The Politics of Economic Stabilization: IMF Standby Programs in Latin America, 1954–1984," *Comparative Politics*, Vol. 19, No. 1 (October 1986), pp. 1–24.

[12] Giovanni Andrea Cornia, Richard Jolly, and Frances Stewart, eds., *Adjustment with a Human Face: Protecting the Vulnerable and Promoting Growth*, Vol. I (Oxford, England: Clarendon Press for the United Nations Children's Fund, 1987). See also UNICEF's annual *Report on the State of the World's Children*, 1988 and 1989.

[13] Recognizing this problem, the World Bank has incorporated in some sector and hybrid loans more effective incentives for "line" or operating agencies. For example, such a loan might incorporate a three-way agreement in which the agency agreed to specific reforms, the World Bank agreed to provide the government with foreign exchange, and the ministry of finance agreed to increase the local currency budget of the operating agency for specified purposes.

[14] C. David Finch, "An IMF Debt Plan," *The International Economy*, Vol. 3, No. 2 (March–April 1989), pp. 89–91; Percy S. Mistry, *African Debt: The Case for Relief for Sub-Saharan Africa* (Oxford, England: Oxford International Associates, 1988), p. 46, paragraph on IMF obligations.

[15] On this third channel, see Gerald K. Helleiner, "Policy-Based Program Lending," op. cit., p. 61.

[16] For contrasting views, see Percy Mistry, *African Debt*, op. cit., p. 41 (suggesting that the World Bank should take the lead and the IMF should minimize its role in Sub-Saharan Africa), and Louis Goreux, "The Fund and the Low-Income Countries," in Richard Feinberg, Catherine Gwin, and contributors, *The Future of the IMF* (New Brunswick, N.J.: Transaction Books in Cooperation with the Overseas Development Council, forthcoming 1989), which recommends closer cooperation enhanced by joint missions and negotiations.

Summaries of Chapter Recommendations

Summaries of Chapter Recommendations

1. The Political Management of Economic Adjustment and Reform
(John Waterbury)

Effective economic adjustment requires overcoming political opposition: The key short and medium-run task is coalition management. The adjustment process in developing countries fairly commonly entails the dissolution or realignment of a coalition based on the military, the public sector, organized labor, and urban, white-collar interests. This coalition is pro-urban if not anti-rural, and it promotes import-substituting industrialization while redistributing income from rural to urban populations and to some degree from richer to poorer urban income strata. The original coalition is typically replaced by one that may still include the military, but that relies more on commercial agriculture, private industrialists, and export sectors. This shift *may* reverse urban bias, reduce the standard of living of those on fixed incomes by engendering inflation, and alienate the intelligentsia.

Every regime's ability to govern is buttressed by a set of allied interests and coalition partners. Consequently any regime undertaking structural adjustment must calculate how the process will affect various members of the coalition. The crucial challenge for the political leadership is to avoid injuring the interests of all coalition members simultaneously.

One way to meet that challenge is to compartmentalize the reform agenda in order to spread the burdens of adjustment over time. Only in the most dire circumstances should devaluation, investment reduction, de-indexing of wages, and the elimination of consumer subsidies all be undertaken at the same time.

The leadership must decide not only who will pay what in what order, but also who will be rewarded and in what order. Austerity reduces room for maneuvering on both sides of the ledger. Faced with dwindling public resources during the adjustment process, leaders may be tempted to shed coalition partners—parts of organized labor, inward-oriented private enterprise, public sector "white elephants," etc. This strategy may be feasible in the short term, but in the longer term, the political risk of isolation, paralysis, and loss of power to those pushed out of the coalition is very real.

Therefore, it may make political sense for the leadership to use more resources on coalition maintenance early than to risk isolation or retaliation later. Governments may use three types of rewards to attract or retain constituents:

- Policies and programs that provide incentives for economic actors needed to lead adjustment;
- Partial compensatory payments to those disadvantaged by adjustment;
- Rents and spoils to state officials and private sector allies.

Outside observers, donors, and creditors should be sensitive to these issues and tolerate a range of discretionary and compensatory measures as long as these do not entail excessive rent-seeking or market distortion.

The adjustment process is one of administered hardship, and the distribution of losses should not be transparent. Only measures meant to encourage economic actors to act in new ways should be as visible and consistent as possible, since their intent is to reward certain kinds of behavior. To minimize opposition, governments may need to downplay or obfuscate losses and benefits that result from reforms but do not serve as important economic signals. Donors should recognize that these tactical needs may override their preferences for clear and unambiguous statements of objectives, the explicit elaboration of the measures designed to achieve them, a binding timetable, and a public commitment to the package.

2. Economic Adjustment in New Democracies (Stephan Haggard and Robert R. Kaufman)

In many new democracies, the debt crisis has produced severe social strains, political polarization, and a general erosion of faith in the capacity of government. These conditions are inimical to the consolidation of democratic values and institutions. If new governments are unable to reignite economic growth or are lured toward policies that generate new economic crises, military and anti-democratic social forces—on both right and left—could expand their influence. The current trend toward democratization could slow, or even reverse.

An analysis of fiscal and monetary policy in twenty-five Asian, African, and Latin American countries shows that *established* democracies performed about as well as authoritarian regimes in implementing stable macroeconomic policies during the 1980s. This suggests that domestic support for cautious macroeconomic policies can be built under democratic auspices. As a group, however, *new* (or renewed) democratic governments had particular difficulties in controlling fiscal and monetary policy. These difficulties were partly attributable to the economic legacies that incoming governments inherited from their authoritarian predecessors. These legacies varied widely among the new democracies, but high inflation in a number of Latin American countries compounded both the economic and political problems of maintaining coherent macroeconomic policy.

Political factors also help explain *differences* in performance among the new democracies. High levels of political mobilization during the transition, weak institutions for channeling societal interests, discontinuities in policymaking authority, and populist leadership strategies increase the difficulties in implementing coherent policy. Given that such basic political variables are not manipulable, the policy challenge is to enhance the prospects for democracy while also achieving the objective of stable macroeconomic policies.

In countries facing particular economic and political challenges, aid donors, creditors, and international financial institutions should accept a gradualist approach to stabilization, realistically assess the financial implications of such gradualism, and support phased structural reforms that reduce political risks to new democratic leaders. Creditors should remain open to policy experimentation. In high-inflation settings, wage and price controls may not only help to break cycles of inertial inflation but also ease the struggle for income shares that accompanies rapid price increases—and thus ameliorate the political conditions that sustain inflation. Where inflation has been tamed, the risks of expansionist policies should not be exaggerated. As the case of the Philippines suggests, providing additional assistance may help consolidate new or renewed democracies.

While supporting gradualism and policy experimentation, donors must be alert to the tendency of new democracies to avoid the fiscal and monetary restraint required to make such programs succeed over the longer run. Tough conditionality is thus wholly appropriate, but assistance and relief must at the same time be adequate to generate improved economic performance. Without such a prospect, democratic leaders will face overwhelming political challenges.

Outside creditors must be alert to how increased executive autonomy during periods of political transition can create "honeymoons" during which structural reforms can be launched. New democratic governments and their external supporters should capitalize on the failures of outgoing governments. Government interventions associated with corruption and mismanagement are easier to dismantle during transition periods than during settings of "politics as usual."

Honeymoons

3. Democratization and Disinflation: A Comparative Approach (Laurence Whitehead)

Most regimes in contemporary Latin America can be described as more or less fragile or incipient democracies afflicted with endemic and potentially uncontrolled inflation. In the short term, there is almost no realistic prospect of establishing fully secure modern democracies with stable currencies. But this ideal remains a powerful long-term aspiration. There is a considerable debate about how Latin America's fragile democracies might eventually become "consolidated." There is also a separate and substantial literature on how to move from high inflation to durable price stability. This chapter suggests that there are structural affinities between the two processes that make it worthwhile to consider them in tandem. Moreover, from the practical point of view, the two goals are most likely to prove attainable if each is approached by methods that take into account the requirements of the other.

In countries where democracy is secure, it may be possible to concentrate political energies on a quick and decisive victory over inflation. In countries where price stability is well-entrenched, it may be possible to concentrate similar energies on a process of democratic consolidation. But in most of Latin America, neither of these conditions holds. In such cases, democratization-with-disinflation is most likely to be approached by partial and incremental advances on both fronts. Solid and durable success cannot be achieved until underlying political and economic expectations have been lastingly remolded. This is likely to take at least a decade. In the meantime, the design, pace, style, timing, and sequencing of concrete policies should take into account the impact on both types of expectations.

Both democratic consolidation and disinflation require the collaboration of a wide range of potentially antagonistic socioeconomic and political groupings. In most circumstances, such collaboration will be enhanced by gradualism and consultation. Although "shock treatment" and a resort to highly centralized and secretive decision-making may appear to have some short-term advantages (and may be unavoidable in real crises), continual resort to such methods of policymaking undermines their effectiveness and creates destabilizing expectations.

The establishment or restoration of democracy after a period of authoritarian rule almost always requires some policies of economic redistribution or rectification. Yet most successful stabilization policies involve at least a temporary *postponement* of distributive measures until macroeconomic imbalances have been corrected. At any one moment, these two priorities may seem irreconcilable. However, if both disinflation and democratization are viewed as long-term incremental projects, it may be possible gradually to mitigate the inherent tensions. Either too much immediate redistribution *or* too much sacrifice on the altar of price stability can destabilize politico-economic expectations. A much more positive climate of opinion may be created by the demonstration that demands postponed now can result in a more orderly satisfaction of claims later.

Consequently the most democratic (and also the most credible) disinflation goal is not absolute price stability in the near future, but a progressively more stable price system over a period of years. In practice, this may mean tolerating low double-digit inflation for a long time. However, if policymakers are to be successfully gradualist about disinflation, they must be very firm and consistent in their opposition to inflationary acceleration. The record suggests that most established democracies are reasonably consistent on this (certainly no worse than most dictatorships). It is in the immediate post-democratization period that the risk is greatest of an uncontrolled upsurge of inflation—especially where the transition from authoritarian rule has taken the form of a "rupture" rather than a "pact."

In recent years, the international environment for democratization and disinflation has been far less favorable for Latin America than, say, for the new democracies of Southern Europe. Nevertheless there are intermittent programs of external support. Steady, long-term multilateral policies are required to make it clear that primary responsibility lies with domestic agents acting on their own account. Imposed rather than mutually agreed economic interventions (and even more so political intrusions) should be avoided. International actors need self-restraint to avoid further destabilizing internal expectations.

4. The Politics of Pro-Poor Adjustment
(Joan M. Nelson)

Protecting the poor in the course of adjustment has won much higher priority within developing countries and in international circles as the social costs of the debt crisis and economic depression have mounted. More pro-poor adjustment programs are also being urged as a means of containing rising popular political resistance to the painful side-effects of stabilization and adjustment measures.

But governments usually have little political incentive to help the poor, roughly defined as the poorest third of the population. The measures that are easiest politically are often those which offer only temporary relief (which tend to have substantial foreign funding). Reforms entailing larger, more obvious, and/or permanent shifts of resources from the better off to the poorer are much more difficult. Moreover, measures targeted to the poorest third do little to ease the growing political opposition to stabilization and adjustment programs. The most potent opposition comes from vested interests threatened by specific economic reforms and from the "popular sectors" and middle classes which have experienced the heaviest losses during the 1980s.

Therefore, sharply targeted pro-poor measures should be pursued mainly to relieve suffering and promote social justice. Their contribution to political sustainability is likely to be modest. There is some risk that temporary compensatory programs may divert resources and attention from more durable and politically difficult reforms. However, some compensatory programs may also serve as opening wedges or models for longer-term pro-poor efforts. Such effects merit priority, even if that initially entails moving more slowly and on a smaller scale. Continuing dialogue, supported by better country-specific data about the poor and fuller information on experience in other countries, may build a basis for more durable future action even where a government's immediate response is limited.

The poor are seldom active politically, but most governments are somewhat sensitive to pressures from the popular sectors or middle deciles of the income distribution, some of whose interests overlap with those of the poor. The continuing fiscal crisis in most African and Latin American countries has led the World Bank and other international development agencies to stress that subsidies must be targeted and health and education expenditures reoriented to favor the wealthy less and the poor more. In practice, such shifts are likely to benefit not only some of the bottom third, but also the politically more vocal middle deciles. This is a political advantage, not a drawback. Instead of running directly counter to political incentives by pressing for tight targeting to the poor alone, external agencies might most effectively help some among the poor by seeking to iden-tify specific interests shared by poor and middle deciles, and specific policies and programs that benefit both.

The broader political pressures threatening adjustment efforts will not, however, be averted by even the best designed restructuring of social expenditures and compensatory programs. The hard-hit middle deciles increasingly demand adjustment that stresses growth more and austerity less—a demand that calls for major shifts in resource flows between North and South, rather than just within poorer nations.

5. Toward State Capability and Embedded Liberalism in The Third World: Lessons for Adjustment (Thomas M. Callaghy)

Contrary to free-market mythology, the state has always played a central role in economic development—a fact even more true now than during the development of capitalism in Europe in the seven-teenth, eighteenth, and nineteenth centuries. Economic adjustment in the Third World today requires a balanced tension or compromise between state and market forces. Since World War II, Western indus-trial states have worked out such a compromise; the resulting arrangements have been described as "embedded liberalism."

To engage in effective economic adjustment, Third World states need two types of state capabilities—the *technocratic and bureau-cratic* ability to formulate and implement policies that facilitate the economic logic of adjustment, and the *political* ability and freedom to buffer the costs of this process while allowing it to take place. Yet the state institutions and political skills that can produce such a cre-ative "political-economy" balance do not appear automatically when needed as part of some adjustment policy imperative. Such capabili-ties are very unevenly distributed among Third World countries. They result from slow, incremental, and uneven political, social, and economic struggles, and therefore are difficult to "build" or engineer deliberately.

Attempts to encourage orthodox liberal economic adjustment in the Third World have had distinctly limited results so far—in large part because the need for a *balanced tension* between state and mar-ket forces has not been adequately appreciated. It is a lesson we have learned for ourselves but have not been willing to extend to others. This chapter argues that a form of embedded liberalism, backed by adequate state capabilities and resources, needs to be extended to the Third World if mutually beneficial adjustment is to be achieved.

Even states with considerable technocratic and bureaucratic capabilities require a form of embedded liberalism. The experiences of Chile and Mexico are used to illustrate this point. States with fewer capabilities, including most of Sub-Saharan Africa, also require a form of embedded liberalism, but pose still more complex dilemmas as outside agencies try to compensate for technocratic and bureaucratic weaknesses.

Successful economic adjustment also requires adequate resources—but weak state capabilites often limit the external financial assistance that can be used effectively, thereby threatening the sustainability of reform. Inadequate state capabilities affect the scope and speed of adjustment and thus the efficacious operation of policy conditionality. One result is greatly increased tension between Third World governments and external actors, particularly the International Monetary Fund (IMF) and the World Bank. Conditionality must be rationalized and made more creatively flexible, and external actors need to ensure that their efforts to compensate for weak state capability have more lasting effects.

Some external actors, especially the World Bank and, to a lesser degree, the IMF, increasingly recognize the importance of the state and the need to proceed more slowly, carefully, and consistently in attempting to overcome institutional and other political and social obstacles to adjustment. Many Western leaders, treasuries, and legislatures have yet to learn these lessons, however. Above all, they should allow the World Bank and the IMF and their own aid agencies to put into effect the hard-won lessons of the last decade, so that Third World economic reform can become more viable.

6. International Financial Institutions and the Politics of Adjustment (Miles Kahler)

The economic policy changes that external agencies require of national governments in the course of adjustment—known as "conditionality"—remain a source of political contention between governments and their creditors and in the domestic politics of individual countries. Three points of conflict, each with high political content, have been particularly prominent. National governments contest the content of adjustment programs—whether IMF or World Bank policy prescriptions are the correct ones for their particular economies. Governments also resist the intrusion of external agencies as an infringement on the autonomy of their economic policy-making. And domestic groups that stand to lose politically and economically from adjustment policies attempt to slow or halt policy changes through the political process. This record of persistent conflict suggests that—from the point of view of both developing countries and IFIs—better management of the participation of external agencies in the politics of adjustment could produce better results.

The record of decisionmaking and implementation during adjustment programs suggests that external influence significantly affects the sustained direction of economic policy in only a limited number of cases. Deeply divided governments are often so paralyzed that external pressure has little effect; other governments have clearly determined upon a program of economic adjustment before outsiders have provided financial support or advice. Only in a few delicately balanced cases have external agencies appeared to tilt decisions in favor of broad economic reforms. The connection between external involvement and successful implementation is even more tenuous. This record of apparently limited external influence on adjustment outcomes points to a need for strategies that are less politically charged.

Policy dialogue is often recommended as one option for changing the political dynamics of conditionality. Steps that might improve the political prospects for dialogue include: widening discussions beyond a limited technocratic core, shortening and simplifying the list of policy conditions, and possibly raising the political profile of the dialogue. But successful policy dialogue has its own prerequisites, including willingness on the part of IFIs to consider alternative economic diagnoses and programs and to distance themselves from private creditors. The negotiating strategy of external agencies needs to be more sensitive to the *political limits* imposed on their partners in dialogue.

Increased financial resources are often central to the political success of adjustment programs. By increasing the likelihood of rapid resumption of economic growth and providing resources to alter the payoffs in domestic politics, financing provides one means for governments to surmount the political risks of adjustment. But tough conditionality without generous finance is not likely to produce adjustment with growth: In a number of developing countries in the 1980s, stringent policy conditions with limited financial support deepened economic stagnation that undermined confidence in governments and their economic programs. Nor is generous finance alone a guarantee of adjustment with growth. The clearest instances of substantial adjustment and resumed growth were indeed supported by substantial financing, but clearcut political commitment played an equally important role. Successful policy dialogue could help IFIs better assess the degree of political commitment to proposed programs.

Despite the importance of improved "reading" of the politics of adjustment, external agencies probably should not openly engage in political analysis. They could, however, considerably improve their use of information already available to them on the politics of adjustment—beginning with a greater effort to collect and utilize within their own institutions the information that they themselves have gathered over time. The IFIs cannot intervene, or take steps that appear to intervene, in the politics of their member nations. But better analysis of the political problems of adjustment is not political intervention; it is an important contribution to the efficacy of program advice and financial support.

Fragile Coalitions: The Politics of Economic Adjustment

Chapter 1

The Political Management of Economic Adjustment and Reform

John Waterbury

In many respects the task of political management is one of coalition management, as every regime has a set of allied interests and coalition partners that buttress its ability to govern. Consequently any regime undertaking structural adjustment must calculate how the process will affect various members of the coalition. Coalitions vary from country to country and over time,[1] but at any point in the reform process, some coalition members stand to lose or gain more than others. The crucial challenge for the political leadership is to avoid injuring the interests of all coalition members simultaneously. That may sound obvious, but the adjustment process often is undertaken during, and because of, deep economic crisis—when far-reaching reforms have to be initiated quickly and across the board. All that may save the regime is the fact that the level of economic distress is already very high. In August 1983, in the depths of drought, Senegal raised consumer prices, froze civil service salaries and hiring, lowered producer prices for groundnuts, and imposed an emergency tax on the public payroll to relieve the drought-stricken countryside. No leader would ever want to take on such a broad array of interests voluntarily. Senegal's President Abdou Diouf, however, had his back to the wall—a posture that anticipatory reform might have helped avoid.

The general propositions and lessons adduced in this chapter draw upon the experiences of six countries in the Middle East and one neighbor, Pakistan, that are contemplating or have undertaken structural adjustment reforms. These countries face two broad sets of challenges—one social, the other bureaucratic—in the adjustment process. The social challenge, on which this chapter will focus, encompasses the issue of the distribution of the costs and benefits of reforms and the likely responses of affected groups in society. The second challenge, which will receive somewhat less attention, relates to different bureaucratic interests and how they respond to the task of implementing (or sabotaging) reforms. In both instances, what is being sought is radically different behavior on the part of groups and individuals that have become accustomed to patterns no longer deemed appropriate—and thus have developed vested interests in perpetuating the status quo. As we shall see, structural adjustment may affect the resources available to bureaucratic interests as well as their accustomed behavior, and in such cases coalition issues are at stake.

Coalition Size

Theoretically, coalition leaders should strive to reduce the size of coalitions to limit and concentrate the resources needed to maintain them. The smaller the coalition and the more compatible the interests of its components, the lower the level of resources needed to maintain it. In times of austerity this maxim would appear to be especially valid. Thus a military dictatorship, run by and for the military, illustrates a very small and internally successful coalition.

It may be posited that coalitions usually will have to be larger than the size necessary to win in any specific situation—simply because political and economic situations constantly change. The degree of incompatibility of interests within coalitions will increase with size, as will the amount of resources required to hold them together. Careful use of sequential rewards and punishments will be required to service them. Thus the leadership's challenge is to decide not only who will pay what in what order, but also who will be rewarded and in what order. Austerity reduces room for maneuver on both sides of the ledger. Squeaking wheels will get the grease, and with that in mind, leaders must retain considerable discretionary control over resource allocation. The kind of automaticity that the donor community and technical economists crave may have to be partially sacrificed. Specific examples of this dynamic will be provided later in this chapter. At this point it should only be noted that certain kinds of discretionary resource allocation must be seen as necessary to the success of structural adjustment.

Faced with dwindling public resources during the adjustment process, leaders may be tempted to shed coalition partners—segments of organized labor, inward-oriented private enterprises, public sector "white elephants," etc. Turkey has been moving in this direction since 1983, and it may be that Algeria, in the wake of the fall 1988 riots, is following a similar strategy in an authoritarian setting. This strategy may be feasible in the short term, but in the longer term the political risk of isolation, paralysis, and loss of power to those pushed out of the coalition is very real.

In sum, it may make political sense for the leadership to use more resources on coalition maintenance early than to risk isolation or retaliation later. One can conceive of the reward system to all constituencies as consisting of three kinds of expenditures. The first are outlays designed to support the adjustment process and to send positive signals to economic actors who are to benefit from and lead the process. The second are compensatory payments to those who will be disadvantaged by the process (although compensation cannot be equivalent to the full extent of the loss). Third are resources absorbed in rents and spoils. Donors, creditors, and economic advisors approve of the first, do not always understand the logic of the second, and condemn the third. It is in fact the design and disbursement of compensatory payments that is crucial to transitional periods in coalition management. For example, periodic but non-comprehensive wage increases, temporary subsidies for specific goods, investment in strategically targeted infrastructure and public housing, or, as in Turkey, rebates paid to consumers on the value-added tax, are typical compensatory mechanisms.

Coalition Composition and the Nature of Defection

The seven countries under consideration in this chapter have coalitions of varying composition. Table 1 provides a very tentative identification of coalition members and nonmembers, along with an equally tentative estimate of their weight in the coalition.

No matter how approximate our estimates, there is considerable variation among the seven countries in terms of the components of the dominant coalition. In none, however, can the peasantry be said to carry much weight. Algeria's *secteur auto-géré* (worker self-managed farms set up on properties abandoned by French settlers in 1962) was once a partial exception, but in 1987 it was effectively leased out to private cultivators. While the civil service in all of these countries with the possible exception of Jordan is large and expensive, it is too sprawling and internally stratified to act corporately.

All other categories show significant variability, the least occurring with respect to the military. In six of the seven countries, the military plays an important role in all public affairs and in policymaking. In all seven, it absorbs a large part of public expenditures and scarce foreign exchange (Egypt's military debt alone is $4.5 billion). Moreover, in Algeria, Egypt, and to a lesser extent Morocco, the armed forces control their own economic undertakings, producing goods and providing

Table 1. Potential and Actual Components of Dominant Coalitions

Component	Algeria	Egypt	Jordan	Morocco	Tunisia	Pakistan	Turkey
Organized Labor	N	S	A	N	S-N	N	S-N
Peasantry	A	A	A	A	A	A	A
Capitalist Farmers	A	N	S	S	S	S	S
Civil Service	N	N	N	N	N	N	N
Public Sector Managers	S	S	W	S	N	N	N
Private Importers	A	S	–	S	–	N-S	N-S
Private Exporters	A	W	S	S	S	N	S
ISI[a] Manufacturing	S	S	W	N	N	N	N-S
The Military	S	S	S	S	W	S	S

Note: A = Absent; not part of the coalition. N = Neutral; present but of indeterminate strength. S = Strong. W = Weak.
[a] Import-substituting industrialization.

Source: Author's estimates.

services that occasionally invade the civilian economy. Only Tunisia has so far kept the military within manageable political and economic proportions. The removal of President Habib Bourguiba in 1987 for reasons of health and his replacement by General Zine al-Abidine Ben Ali clearly raises the profile of the military in Tunisia, but it is far too early to know whether or not its weight in the coalition will change.

The place of organized labor in coalition politics is difficult to assess. Of the seven countries, only Pakistan and Jordan do not have a tradition of powerful labor confederations. The others do possess such confederations, but they have all been subordinated to some extent to the administration and the public enterprise sector. In Egypt, for example, the giant General Confederation of Labor has been described as a "veto group,"[2] able to trade labor discipline in exchange for preferred policies (e.g., no joint ventures between public sector enterprises and foreign capital). In Morocco, the labor movement has splintered over the years into rival confederations among which the UMT *(Union Marocaine du Travail)*, with its aging leadership, is still predominant. As in Algeria, unauthorized strikes appear to have increased over the last decade. In Turkey, the military takeover of September 1980 led to the dissolution of the leftist Revolutionary Workers' Union Confederation (DISK) labor confederation, leaving the field to the main labor confederation, Türk-İş, whose membership was heavily concentrated in the public sector. Similarly, in Pakistan the late Field Marshal Zia ul-Haq clipped the wings of unionized labor, which had been part of Zulfikar Ali Bhutto's coalition.

In several of these countries, as in many other developing countries, corporatist labor arrangements that encourage labor cooperation with government policies are being put under severe strain. Reduced public investment budgets, cuts in consumer subsidies, and reductions in welfare services have broken social pacts elaborated over decades of state-led, import-substituting industrialization. The leaderships of the key labor organizations are experiencing great difficulty in holding the rank and file in check and may be tempted to bolster their own images and to jockey for top positions by leading or following their workers into strikes. The national political leadership must be prepared to make concessions to labor in the application of austerity programs—if for no other reason than to enhance the credibility of their own coopted labor leaders.

While the peasantry is missing from all seven coalitions, market-oriented capitalist farmers are present in six, strong in five, and absent only in Algeria—although with the breakup of the *secteur auto-géré*, that situation may be changing. In Jordan, Morocco, Tunisia, and Turkey these groups play an important part in generating agricultural exports as well as in producing commodities for middle- and upper-income consumers in domestic markets. They can be important supporters of adjustment programs, and because many urban elite members, including the military, have commercial agricultural interests, the anti-urban impact of pro-agrarian reforms may be mitigated—at least for some important coalition members. Jordan has become an important supplier of agricultural produce to the oil-exporting countries of the Middle East; Morocco and Tunisia are struggling desperately for market niches in the European Economic Community; and Pakistan has the potential to become a major grain exporter.

Over the long term, winning the cooperation of public sector managers for the reform program will be crucial. In all seven countries, the public sector carries considerable weight in terms of assets owned, people employed, sectors in which it is present, and control over foreign exchange earnings (especially from the marketing of oil, natural gas, phosphates, citrus, etc.). Egypt and Algeria, however, boast the largest and most diversified public sectors, which dwarf all private sector activity outside of agriculture. Public sector managerial elites are well entrenched in the coalitions of all but Jordan; and in Egypt and Algeria they are in a position to influence—if not shape—macro policy. The challenge here for the political leadership is to restructure incentives for public sector managers to encourage new forms of behavior. Ending public sector monopolies and monopsonies, lowering tariffs, deregulating prices, and providing for real management autonomy at the firm level may produce the desired overall effect. Senior management, however, may prefer early retirement to the distress of learning new tricks.

Private importers—in contrast to the parastatal trading companies that are present in all seven countries—play an important role in the dominant coalitions of at least three of these countries: Egypt, Morocco, and Pakistan. In Egypt, the press frequently talks about the "Mafia of the importers"; and since the mid-1970s and the implementation of the own-exchange system, under which importers were no longer required to account for the source of their foreign exchange, importers have handled billions of dollars' worth of business each year. They are accused of willfully stifling local industry by introducing competing imports (e.g., cement, textiles), of trafficking illegally in foreign exchange and drugs, and of bringing down government ministers who try to regulate their activities.

With the exception of Jordan, all of the countries under consideration have important public and private enterprises that evolved in an era of import-substituting industrialization. In Egypt and Algeria, most of these are concentrated in the public sector, and their managers possess the bureaucratic bargaining skills necessary to hold off or deflect reforms aimed at increasing their competitiveness and efficiency. In Egypt, managers appear to have used those skills, while in Algeria the reform process has advanced significantly. Trade liberalization and devaluation will tend to hurt these enterprises, whether public or private, by lowering effective rates of protection and raising the costs of imports. They may respond with uncontrolled borrowing from the banking system, divestment, or running down their assets.[3]

All of the coalition members mentioned here are defined by function or the nature of their economic activity. In many countries, however, there are coalition members that also may be defined by ethnic origin, religious status, or regional background. (One thinks, for instance, of the role played by the Kikuyu in the dominant coalition of Kenya.) Among the seven countries considered here, such factors are of marginal importance in all but two: Turkey and Pakistan. The cleavage between Palestinians and those of Bedouin origin in Jordan may have implications for the implementation of reforms (by way of simplistic example, non-Palestinian Jordanians dominate the officers corps, while Palestinians are more active in trade, industry, and white-collar professions). Some have argued that there is a "Berber question" in Algeria,[4] but the presence of Algerians of Berber origin in all of the components of the coalition suggests that this is not an issue. Turkey and Pakistan, in contrast, face claims from major ethno-regional groups (e.g., Kurds, Sindhis, etc.) that are excluded from their dominant coalitions.

All seven countries are in varying degrees Muslim, and in each the issue of "Islamic economics" is very much an item on the political and policy agenda. Pakistan has gone the furthest in adopting an "Islamic" economy. By and large, in Pakistan and elsewhere, this boils down to interest-free banking and finance. What else may be distinctive in Islamic economic arrangements is not at all clear. What is clear is that self-conscious Muslim groups have become identifiable constituencies in these countries, and parts of them have been or might be incorporated within dominant coalitions. In Turkey, Pakistan, and Egypt the political leadership has taken on an Islamic patina at the same time that an important Islamic opposition has been permitted.

Bargaining with Islamic interests in the economic domain typically revolves around the issue of the legality of interest. Throughout the region, Islamic banking has been established alongside more conventional financial institutions. This development has important implications for the adjustment process. Standard measures to promote adjustment and resource switching (toward foreign exchange earning or saving) by recalibrating relative interest rates may have their impact blunted. Efforts to promote long-term private investment may be thwarted by the tendency of Islamic institutions to use their funds in quick-return, sometimes speculative, investments.[5] We have also seen the emergence of novel financial intermediaries. In Egypt, scores of Islamic finance companies *(sharikat tawzif al-amwal)* have proliferated, with the largest holding several billion dollars in local currency or foreign exchange. Their asset base, to the extent that it is known, is narrow, but the rate of return on deposits has been well in excess of the rate of inflation and far ahead of the interest paid by public and private banks. Only in the summer of 1988 were steps taken by the stock exchange board to regulate these companies. There is little doubt that several highly placed Egyptians have been associated with these companies. In Turkey, Prime Minister Turgut Özal has built up a number of off-budget funds whose total worth is on the order of $5–7 billion. They are fed by various import levies and earmarked taxes, and their annual investments (mainly in housing and infrastructure) reached 6 per cent of gross domestic product (GDP) in 1988. In short, the spread of Islamic financing—in part to satisfy Muslim constituents and coalition members—removes a non-negligible part of the economy of some of these countries from the reach of conventional adjustment policies.

Threats and Defection

A fairly common pattern in developing countries is that the adjustment process entails the dissolution, or at least the realignment, of a dominant coalition based on the military, the public sector, organized labor, and urban, white-collar interests. This coalition is pro-urban, if not anti-rural, and it attempts to promote import-substituting industrialization while redistributing income from rural to urban populations and from richer to poorer income strata. Because its rhetoric is often populist and nationalist, it is likely to receive the support of the intelligentsia. This coalition is often replaced by one that may still include the military but that relies more on commercial agriculture, private industrialists, and export sectors. It may reverse urban bias, harm the standard of living of those on fixed incomes (through removal of consumer subsidies and increased rates of inflation), and alienate the intelligentsia. Distributional programs are deemphasized, while economic efficiency and international competitiveness become the new coalition's watchwords. As different coalition members and non-coalition sectors of society experience the distress of adjustment, they possess varying degrees of potential to disrupt the process through strikes (organized labor); through riots (urban unorganized and low-income groups); through capital flight (private sector, importers); through remittance witholding (migrant and skilled labor); and through hoarding and unsecured borrowing (public sector enterprise).

The most important aspect of these threats—the "thresholds" at which they are most likely to be activated—is the one about which the least is known. Political leaders must gauge when injuring the interests of specific groups will trigger a disruptive response. Experience has varied so widely that no satisfying answers are available. In several countries, within and outside the Middle East, wage earners have suffered substantial losses in real income over several years. In Mexico, about 200,000 industrial jobs have been lost since 1982. Organized labor and white-collar associations have not impeded the austerity measures that produced these results. Over the same period, Mexico has experienced major capital flight—while Turkey, in much the same economic circumstances, has not. Such cases suggest that thresholds are often unexpectedly high. But there are also contrary cases: Algeria's authoritarian regime was challenged and shaken in October 1988 by massive riots involving all segments of the population, followed by Jordan's similar crisis in the spring of 1989.

With this in mind, let us consider the nature of the threats that coalition members and non-coalition members may pose. Organized labor, for example, is generally concentrated in the most advanced and sometimes the most sensitive sectors of the economy. If unions go on strike, they can paralyze rail transport and ports and close down strategic industries, as occurred in some Egyptian military factories in 1968 and in the Iranian oil fields in 1978–79. Failing to anticipate the grievances of a specific union may exact a high political price: The strike of Peru's Guardia Civil in February 1975 not only put an end to the country's stabilization program but eventually undercut the military regime itself; and in Sudan in March 1985, white-collar unions and professional associations were instrumental in bringing down the regime of Gaafar Nimeiri. If strikes by organized labor appear likely, the leadership must try to make sure that labor's grievances do not feed into those of other groups—students, the unemployed, or informal sector labor.

Unorganized labor, the urban unemployed, and shantytown dwellers may be the most violence-prone sectors of the population and the least protected against sudden increases in the cost of living. The results are sometimes spectacular, as in Egypt in January 1977, Casablanca in 1965 and 1981, and Algiers in the fall of 1988. The violence may not be sustained, however, unless it attracts other participants or ties into other causes. A regime may be able to ride out the storm if organized labor has been given some cushion against the impact of the reforms. While Bienen and Gersovitz are probably right in asserting that stabilization and adjustment programs do not usually *cause* violence and instability, it is no less the case that they may ignite an already explosive situation.[6] If the police cannot be used against the rioters (as in Peru in 1975) or if the economic grievances of urban populations become bound up with a religious or ideological movement (as in Iran in 1978 and 1979), the violence may become self-sustaining and draw in ever larger segments of the populace. Similarly, movements that initially may appear marginal or extremist can suddenly find willing recruits if economic hardship is abruptly imposed on a given sector of the urban population.

Austerity combined with devaluation may provoke capital flight. This is the threat or weapon of the private sector—particularly importers, financial services firms, and foreign exchange brokers. Capital flight in anticipation of a devaluation can cause more damage than a reform program may be able to correct. Economists can debate the relative merits of a quick and significant devaluation without prior warning, a series of mini-devaluations, or, as Egypt announced in 1986 and then retracted after eighteen months, a "unification of exchange rates." If importers and bankers are important constituents of the coalition, however, the regime may not be able to control what amounts to sabotage of an important facet of the adjustment process. In 1982 Mexico was driven to nationalize much of the private banking sector to try to stop the U.S. dollar hemorrhage.

While migrant labor has not been a formal or recognized component of a dominant coalition in any country, it has shored up the foreign exchange balances of most of the countries examined in this chapter. This is least the case for Algeria, which has relied on rents from gas and petroleum exports, and most the case for Jordan, where remittances have sometimes been the equivalent of two-thirds of gross domestic product (GDP). How devaluation affects remittance flows is of vital importance. Because of the downturn in the region's oil-based economies, a stagnation in remittances in the coming years is likely; but it is possible that, through devaluation and higher interest rates, a greater *proportion* of total remittances may be drawn into the formal banking system in the labor-exporting countries. A strong economic and *political* case for devaluation can be made on these grounds alone. That Algeria in recent years has attracted as little as $140 million in remittances (in comparison to the $2–3 billion earned by Egypt or Turkey) suggests the potential impact of a change in these flows.

Public sector enterprises and their managers may react in a number of ways. In anticipation of devaluation, they may hoard imported raw materials and capital goods, adding to the already-strong run on existing foreign exchange reserves, and they may defy investment cutbacks by borrowing heavily from the public banking system or by defaulting on existing debt.

It is frequently argued that the agrarian sector stands to benefit from structural adjustment, and that only the perpetuation of the status quo of adverse terms of domestic trade for that sector would lead to lower production and flight from "government" crops. That in fact was the case in Turkey between 1980 and 1987, as large increases in domestically produced agricultural inputs, especially fertilizer, were passed on to the agricultural sector. Only specific subsectors engaged in agricultural exports were able to hold their own against the deteriorating terms of trade.[7] Likewise, elimination of indirect subsidies on diesel fuel and electricity could lead to sharp rises in the costs of production, which would have to be either absorbed by the cultivators themselves, with unpredictable consequences, or passed on to consumers, with an equally unpredictable outcome.

How the agrarian sector will be affected by the adjustment process is a matter for empirical investigation. As in Turkey (and also Mexico), the process may initially entail a marked *deterioration* in the overall well-being of the farm sector as prices of inputs soar and liberalized trade regimes open the door to competitive imports of agricultural products. Only specialized agricultural exporters may benefit in the initial stages of adjustment.

The dynamics of coalition restructuring and the implementation of adjustment can be better grasped by examining two contrasting cases. In the 1960s, Turkey and Egypt had roughly similar dominant coalitions. Both countries had followed strategies of import-substituting industrialization (ISI) led by state enterprise. The coalition core consisted of top military leaders, the upper echelons of the state bureaucracy and public enterprise managers, the major labor confederations, and substantial parts of the intelligentsia. In Egypt more than in Turkey, the ISI strategy had a marked anti-rural bias.

By the mid-1970s, both countries were mired in balance-of-payments, debt-servicing, and fiscal crises. They dealt with these crises in radically different ways. In the late 1970s, Egypt was able to capture rents from petroleum exports, Suez Canal fees, and worker remittances. It also obtained strategic rents from the United States as a result of the Camp David Accords. It used these rents to maintain its large, existing ISI-based coalition. The external resources that might have gone into structural adjustment itself and the attendant remaking of the dominant coalition were used instead to sustain the consumption of the existing coalition and to add to it at least one new member: private sector interests in imports and banking. At the close of the 1980s, this formula no longer appears economically sustainable. Rents have declined while the claims of coalition partners have expanded, but the productive structure of the Egyptian economy has not been significantly altered. Only the continued infusion of strategic rents may save Egypt from a painful and disruptive process of coalition shedding and reconstruction.

Turkey, in contrast, had no oil to export and was already suffering from stagnant remittance flows in the late 1970s. Its last two civilian governments in that decade attempted to implement parts of an adjustment package, including devaluation, and Turkey's NATO allies provided a large capital infusion to cushion the process. But due to uncontrolled domestic political violence, the Turkish military seized power in

September 1980 and began a process of draconian reshaping of the dominant coalition. University faculties, student organizations, and labor unions were purged of radical leadership, politicians were arrested, and political parties were dissolved. New legislation sharply curtailed permissible political activities. Once civilian rule was restored in 1983, a new constellation of coalition partners had begun to emerge. The key actors in the adjustment process were to be major private interests coaxed into the export drive, a chastened labor confederation concentrated in the public sector, a demoralized public enterprise sector cut off from public investment, a new financial technocracy to manage the adjustment process, networks of private interests relying on domestic markets and tied as quasi-clients to the regime and the dominant party, and of course the military. The losers in this were urban salaried and white-collar groups, the intelligentsia, and to some extent smallholder farmers, who were victimized by sharp increases in the prices of inputs.

An important lesson to be drawn from these contrasting cases is that continuity and discontinuity in the operation of the regime, rather than the relative degrees of democracy or authoritarianism, set the limits of what is and is not possible in promoting adjustment. Hosni Mubarak, legatee of a quarter-century of regime continuity, is stuck with a coalition that he cannot abandon, and he does not have the resources to build new interests that would support his efforts to pursue adjustment. The Turkish military dissolved or cowed coalition members in Turkey and (having created a political vacuum through the abolition of political parties) left Prime Minister Özal to construct a new coalition of political and economic interests.

The Phasing of Adjustment

A description of two phases of a hypothetical reform and adjustment program can show how the sequencing of reforms may distribute burdens and rewards across potential and actual coalition members over time. It must be stressed that this sequence is illustrative and does not suggest a preferred path. Proper economic sequencing is the subject of an abundant literature.[8] It should also be noted that it is assumed that the beginning of an adjustment program entails fairly standard stabilization measures of the IMF variety, and that such measures will involve more than efforts to bring down inflation.

Phase I

In this phase, the three policy components will be devaluation, deficit reduction through curtailed public investment, and de-indexing wages. The objectives are to protect the devaluation by holding the domestic rate of inflation below that of major trading partners. The reduction in public investment and the de-indexing of wages will serve this purpose. The measures should lead to the promotion of agricultural and manufactured exports. They may promote greater efficiency in public sector performance, and, as the Indian case showed after 1973,[9] reducing investment in import-reliant public sector enterprises lowers imports significantly.

The possible beneficiaries in this hypothetical coalition in Phase I would be agricultural exporters (that is, cultivators already heavily involved in capitalist farming); private, and perhaps public, exporters of manufactured goods; the tourist sector; and migrant workers who would be able to convert their earnings at the new devalued exchange rate.

The potential losers in Phase I are public sector firms (reduced investment flows, restrictions on imports); any firms reliant on imported inputs; the military, which may see the cost of imported armaments rise dramatically; and the construction sector, which will feel the impact of curtailed public investment.

The consequences of Phase I may be neutral or indeterminate for urban populations on low and/or fixed incomes, because the increase in the cost of living induced by the devaluation and the de-indexing of wages may be offset by (a) the higher value in local currency of remitted earnings from abroad, (b) the anti-inflationary impact of reduced government spending, and (c) the maintenance of consumer subsidies.

Phase II

The policy measures associated with this phase are: a reduction in consumer subsidies, the freeing up of agricultural producer prices, lower interest rates, an increase in public investment, some deregulation of industrial prices, tariff reduction, and constant adjustments in the exchange rate.

The goal of these measures is to maintain a moderate rate of growth and avoid stagflation, stimulate agricultural production in general and agricultural exports in particular, encourage private sector investments and a shift toward export markets, create nonagricultural jobs to protect incomes in the nonagricultural sector, and to absorb returning migrant workers.

The beneficiaries of this phase will be the agricultural sector in general—and exporters in particular—and public sector enterprises selling mainly to the domestic market. Having been streamlined in Phase I, these firms will now benefit from increased investment flows.

Phase II will have a neutral or indeterminate impact on public or private import-substituting industries, as they will experience rising costs of domestic inputs and probably of wage bills, which may or may not be offset by easier borrowing and the deregulation of prices. So too will those engaged in the export of manufactured goods experience a rise in the costs of labor and domestic raw materials.

Most trade liberalization measures are saved for the second phase. It is often recommended that these be undertaken at the beginning of a structural adjustment program, but caution is required in the cases of Egypt, Tunisia, Morocco, Pakistan, and Jordan. These five countries have maintained chronic trade imbalances for many years. Sweeping trade liberalizations would aggravate those imbalances before domestic actors could respond in any meaningful way. Turkey—which has gone further than any country in the region in liberalizing trade and promoting exports—has in fact increased its overall level of protection in the last three years through tariffs and levies. Algeria, which in the long run might benefit most from trade liberalization, is the least prepared to deal with the challenge in the short run.

The point of this exercise is not to suggest that these two phases (which do lead to expenditure control and switching) represent the best way to proceed, but rather to illustrate how the reform agenda can be timed to spread the burdens of adjustment without harming the bulk of coalition members simultaneously. Only under the most dire circumstances should devaluation, investment reduction, de-indexing wages, and the elimination of consumer subsidies all be undertaken at the same time.

Tactics: Political Timing, Policy Packaging, Rhetoric and Style, and Credibility

Joan Nelson and others have stated that the adjustment process requires a high degree of elite cohesion and the ability of the elite to project a determination to stay with the process.[10] Only with credibility and predictability will adjustment policies bring about the kind of factor switching and new economic behavior that is desired. Some regimes enjoy that kind of credibility to a greater extent than others, but when hardship is being imposed, elites that are seen by their own people as corrupt or living beyond their means may not have the will or the confidence to ignore the challengers to the reforms. Moreover, elites and coalitions may be badly divided by the very adoption of a structural adjustment program: Thus Indira Gandhi's devaluation of the rupee in 1966, for example, placed severe strains on her ruling coalition. The riots in Algeria in the fall of 1988 clearly placed similar pressures on Chadli Benjedid's coalition, which is now undergoing a major restructuring.

Democracy may well be of very practical benefit to regimes undertaking painful economic measures. In the Middle East, countries as different as Turkey and Israel have succeeded in implementing or sustaining tough austerity measures despite coalition governments or governments enjoying very narrow majorities. Two electoral scenarios are possible. In the first, leaders go to the people for a general endorsement and then, backed by a fresh mandate, push through the adjustment package. Abdou Diouf was elected President of Senegal in March 1983 and pressed through his austerity package the following August. Turgut Özal has followed somewhat the same path since the first victory of his Motherland Party in 1983. The strategy can backfire, however; the 1977 riots in Egypt came after the parliamentary elections of November 1976. A given regime may want to make the adjustment program an open issue in the election—so that an electoral victory can be claimed as a popular mandate to move ahead. It does not appear that the 1987 Egyptian elections were utilized for this purpose.

A second scenario could be to start implementation of the adjustment process and then call elections. The gamble here is that the countryside will have drawn benefits from the reforms and that this block of voters—more numerous than any other constituency in the country—can be mobilized in favor of the regime. Prior to Turkish elections in Fall 1987, Özal pumped over a billion dollars into the countryside through increases in crop purchase prices. This did not bring on a landslide victory, inasmuch as cultivators had not been doing well in previous years, but it did help produce a relative majority of votes cast and a solid majority in the national assembly. Authoritarian regimes cannot so visibly legitimize themselves with the rural majority, but they too have to face concentrated urban constituencies that will have to bear a good deal of the burden of adjustment and that are in a position to sabotage the whole process.

It should be noted, however, that this division by urban and rural is quite artificial—certainly in the countries under consideration. The extent and nature of rural-urban migration is such that the countryside and the city are intimately linked through off-farm employment and remittances. Rural families are not insulated from a downturn in living standards of urban populations. If a regime turns to the countryside for support—perhaps what the Algerian regime is contemplating today—it will have to shift substantial investment resources and price incentives to offset the impact of deteriorating urban standards of living on rural households.

From developing countries the donor community seeks clear and unambiguous statements of objectives, the explicit elaboration of the measures designed to achieve them, a binding timetable, and a public commitment to the package. The adjustment process is one of administered hardship, and the distribution of losses should not be transparent.

Therefore leaders and policymakers should resist pressure to make such public statements. Policies that are meant to send signals to economic actors to encourage them to behave in new ways are of course an exception. These should be as visible and consistent as possible, as their intent is to reward certain kinds of behavior. But austerity policies should be uneven, sometimes internally inconsistent, and if possible camouflaged. Losses and benefits to various constituents should not be made clear. The higher the potential political and economic costs of structural adjustment, the greater the premium on obfuscation. Yair Aharoni captures this dilemma well:

> When goals are in conflict, a clear-cut resolution or the setting of priorities may not be the optimal solution to all actors. Actors will then rather resort to a quasi-resolution of conflicts, defer the exact definition of the problem, or use log-rolling, but will avoid an open confrontation.[11]

One problem that many regimes may have to face is how to contain the appetites of their own military establishments. The Mexicans, from President Lázaro Cárdenas on, have shown how. One way was to publish a substantial outlay for the military in the annual budget and then to underspend year after year by as much as 30 per cent. Another kind of subterfuge has been practiced in Egypt, where subsidies have been maintained on a whole range of items from a certain quality of bread to bus fares but the subsidized items and services themselves have gradually become unavailable, replaced by slightly modified but costlier ones. This is de-subsidization by stealth. It does not take food from the mouths of the poor, but it does avoid the kind of anger that might be expressed were prices raised officially.

It was decided in India in February 1986 to reduce subsidies on a number of commodities consumed mainly in the urban areas. Some price increases would primarily affect middle-income consumers, many of whom tended to be supporters of Rajiv Gandhi. The Prime Minister divided his coalition partners by carefully maintaining subsidized electricity rates, fertilizers, and diesel fuel for the market farmers. A few days after the price increases had been announced, delegations from his own party poured into the capital to tell him of the hardship being wrought on their constituents. Having ostentatiously received their grievances, and having demonstrated that his party had its collective finger on the popular pulse, the Prime Minister cut the price increases back by half—thereby proving his concern for the masses and preempting any attacks from the opposition. It is alleged that the Prime Minister had raised prices by twice as much as his advisors thought economically necessary, with the result that his "cuts" merely reduced the increases to the economically optimal level. Whether true or not, the allegation captures the spirit of the staging that the reform process may require. Agile-footed politicians cannot transform an economy facing structural crisis, but probably they alone can survive the reform process.

Thus only in rare circumstances—for example, when a new regime comes to power through a coup or the ballot box—is the leadership likely to be supported by a consensus sufficient to allow it to lay out policy goals and to stick by them without jeopardizing the cohesion of the regime itself. Incumbent regimes, like those of Egypt or Algeria, will inevitably have to trample on the interests of important elements in their coalitions. So far Hosni Mubarak has avoided doing so, and consequently adjustment has been sacrificed. In contrast, Chadli Benjedid has seized upon the riots of October 1988 to purge his own regime and to prepare the ground for a more vigorous push toward reform.[12]

Conclusion

Even in authoritarian systems, structural adjustment will require careful political management of the interests that constitute the regime's basic support coalition. Some resources will have to be used for essentially political purposes, and, because resources are scarce, such utilization will appear wasteful from an economic efficiency point of view. It should not be forgotten, however, that a regime that alienates most or all of its coalition partners will not be able to pursue the adjustment process.

Outside observers, donors, and creditors should be sensitive to these issues. A clear principle can be used as a guideline for the use of public resources: It is legitimate to oppose the use of resources for excessive rent-seeking as well as for market interventions that may be politically motivated and that create major market distortions. At the same time, a range of discretionary practices in resource allocation—especially those that are designed to compensate partially those interests that suffer the most in the adjustment process—should be accepted. Inevitably, many will perceive the process to be inequitable—and it may in fact be so. The political leadership will want to mask as much as possible the real extent of losses—and their precise bearers. Compensatory payments may help to mitigate the impact of adjustment and to sequence the distribution of pain among coalition members and large segments of the population. Forthright declarations of policy intent, the laying out of timetables, and the public targeting of specific interests may well leave leaders without room to maneuver and lead to the defection and opposition of groups vital to regime maintenance.

Notes

[1] Robert Bates, *Markets and States in Tropical Africa: The Political Bases of Agricultural Policies* (Berkeley: University of California Press, 1981).

[2] Robert Bianchi, "The Corporatization of the Egyptian Labor Movement," *Middle East Journal,* Vol. 40, No. 3 (1986), pp. 425–44.

[3] This was the case in Chile in the late 1970s. In 1983, a neo-conservative regime found itself obliged to take over private sector banks crippled by bad debts.

[4] Hugh Roberts, "The Economics of Berberism: The Kabyle Question in Contemporary Algeria," *Government and Opposition,* Vol. 18, No. 2 (1983), pp. 218–35.

[5] Zubair Iqbal and Abbas Mirakhor, *Islamic Banking,* IMF Occasional Paper No. 49 (Washington, D.C.: International Monetary Fund, March 1987).

[6] Henry Bienen and Mark Gersovitz, "Economic Stabilization, Conditionality, and Political Stability," *International Organization,* Vol. 39, No. 1 (1985), pp. 729–54.

[7] Halis Akder, "Turkey's Export Expansion in the Middle East, 1980–1985," *Middle East Journal,* Vol. 41, No. 4 (1987).

[8] R.I. McKinnon, "The Order of Economic Liberalization: Lessons from Chile and Argentina," *Carnegie-Rochester Conference Series on Public Policy,* Vol. 17 (New York: Elselvier, 1982), pp. 159–86.

[9] Montek Ahluwalia, "Balance-of-Payments Adjustment in India, 1970–71 to 1983–84," *World Development,* Vol. 14, No. 8 (1986), pp. 937–62.

[10] Joan Nelson, "The Political Economy of Stabilization: Commitment, Capacity and Public Response," *World Development,* Vol. 12, No. 10 (1984), pp. 938–1006.

[11] Yair Aharoni, *The Evolution and Management of State-Owned Enterprises* (New York: Ballinger, 1986), p. 389; and William Ascher, *Scheming for the Poor: The Politics of Redistribution in Latin America* (Cambridge, Mass.: Harvard University Press, 1984), p. 18.

[12] See John Entelis, "Algeria Under Chadli: Liberalization without Democratization," *Middle East Insight,* Vol. 6, No. 3 (1988), pp. 47–64.

Chapter 2

Economic Adjustment in New Democracies

Stephan Haggard and Robert R. Kaufman

The debt crisis of the 1980s has coincided with a widespread trend toward political liberalization and democratization in the developing world. In the early years of the decade, restive publics in many countries held authoritarian governments responsible for economic difficulties, forcing military rulers to return to the barracks. This left their successors to deal with the divisive demands of economic adjustment while also navigating transitions to democratic rule. In Asia, the Philippines, the Republic of Korea, and Turkey have faced this dual problem of economic and political change. Nigeria, Africa's largest country, is undergoing a phased return to democracy against a backdrop of severe economic crisis. In Latin America, some of the biggest debtors, including Argentina and Brazil, emerged only recently from authoritarian rule and now face new electoral cycles.

In most of these countries, the debt crisis has produced severe social strains, political polarization, and a general erosion of faith in the capacity of government. These conditions are inimical to the consolidation of democratic values and institutions. If new democratic governments are unable to reignite economic growth, or are lured toward policies that generate new economic crises, military and anti-democratic social forces—both right and left—could expand their influence. The current trend toward democratization could slow or even reverse.

This chapter explores how new democracies have coped with one aspect of this economic and political crisis: the problem of formulating fiscal and monetary policy.[1] Macroeconomic policy is by no means the only economic challenge that new democracies face. In many countries, economic recovery will depend on negotiations to reduce debt servicing burdens, as well as on a variety of factors beyond the control of the debtors themselves, such as world interest rates and commodity prices. In addition, not all new democracies face similar problems. Some confront daunting inflation and must urgently address the problem of stabilization, while others have greater leeway for expansionist measures. Nonetheless there is a growing consensus that budget deficits and erratic monetary and exchange-rate policies contributed to the debt crisis of the 1980s. Sustaining coherent fiscal and credit policies will be a crucial component of sustainable economic recovery.[2]

The first section of this chapter outlines some theoretical considerations about the relationship between political regime type and economic policy. The second section presents data from a sample of twenty-five countries, comparing the performance of countries with continuous democracies, authoritarian regimes, and countries that have undergone a democratic transition. The third section focuses on differences among the new democracies themselves. Three findings emerge from our analysis. First, established democracies have performed about as well as authoritarian regimes in implementing stable macroeconomic policies during the 1980s. Second, new democracies as a group did appear to have difficulties controlling fiscal and monetary policy during the period of transition. Third, the *differences* among the new democracies are as striking as the similarities, and must be explained by reference to different political as well as economic circumstances. These include the level of political mobilization during the transition, the degree of institutional continuity, and the coalition-building strategies of incoming executives.

We conclude by offering some prescriptions for conserving or enlarging the prospects for democratic adjustment. Outside donors and international financial institutions must understand that some new democracies face important political constraints in implementing economic policy. In these cases, creditor governments should accept a gradualist approach to stabilization. They should realistically assess the financial implications of such gradualism and support phased structural reforms that reduce political risks to new democratic leaders.

Regime Type and Adjustment: Theoretical Considerations

Recent cross-national research has cast some doubt on the conventional wisdom that authoritarian regimes have a particular advantage in imposing the austerities associated with macroeconomic stabilization.[3] In a study of the International Monetary Fund's (IMF) programs in

Latin America, Karen Remmer found virtually no difference between democratic and authoritarian regimes in their ability to control deficits and expenditures or to restrict the growth of credit.[4] Stephan Haggard's study of thirty IMF Extended Fund Facility programs found that some authoritarian regimes, such as Zaire or Haiti, did poorly at implementation, while certain democracies, such as Sri Lanka, adopted fairly comprehensive adjustment programs.[5] As Barry Ames concludes in a study of fiscal policy in Latin America, "classifying governments as authoritarian or nonauthoritarian oversimplifies: in reality few governments are so secure that the budget is not a tool for increasing support."[6]

These findings do not necessarily imply that regime type is irrelevant to understanding adjustment policy—only that more nuanced distinctions may be required *within* the authoritarian and democratic categories. In "strong" authoritarian regimes, for example, secure chief executives support technocratic decisionmakers and insulate them from distributive pressures.[7] The government maintains a substantial degree of autonomy from domestic political forces in formulating policy, and the capacity of bureaucracies to implement policy is high. In "weak" authoritarian regimes, by contrast, governments are more likely to be unstable. Decisionmaking is poorly organized, technocrats are marginalized, bureaucratic capacity is low, and the state is penetrated by rent-seeking groups. In the worst cases, the line between the public and private spheres blurs entirely, and governments prove incapable of framing or implementing coherent programs of any sort. One might thus expect the performance of authoritarian regimes to exhibit wide variation.

Democratic governments may also be differentiated in various ways, including on the basis of their longevity. New (or renewed) democracies—or "democratic transitions"—are systems that have recently moved toward open elections after prolonged or episodic experience with authoritarian rule. For the 1980s, this category includes (among others) the new regimes in Brazil, Argentina, the Philippines, Turkey, and the Republic of Korea. "Established" democracies, by contrast, are systems in which competitive electoral systems have persisted over some extended period of time, such as India, Colombia, Sri Lanka, and Venezuela.[8]

There are at least three reasons why new (or renewed) democracies may encounter particular problems in pursuing stable macroeconomic policies. First, political transitions typically reflect an increased level of political mobilization and conflict. It is usually because such conflict cannot be overcome through repression that authoritarian regimes weaken and give way to constitutional ones. Because political mobilization generally increases in the last phases of authoritarian rule, it confronts new democratic leaders with previously repressed demands, heightened social and economic expectations, and strong pressures to reward supporters and incoming groups.

Pressures from below are coupled with uncertainties at the top among new political elites. In the immediate post-transition period, the possibility exists that authoritarian political forces will re-enter politics. Short-run macroeconomic policy choices thus not only have coalitional consequences; they may also affect the survival of the new regime itself. These uncertainties shorten the time horizons over which politicians calculate the costs of policy choice. Difficult economic policy actions that create resistance or unrest—and that might provide an excuse for a reversal of the democratization process—are likely to be avoided.

Finally, democratization is likely to involve more substantial turnover in technical personnel and changes in decisionmaking institutions than is the case with changes of government in established democracies. With increased social demands, the uncertainties facing new political leaders, and the technocrats' own interest in supporting the democratic experiment, incoming economic policy teams are more likely to pursue expansionist programs that meet expectations and reduce social conflict in the short run.

Conditions in established democracies can be expected to differ from those in new democracies in several ways. Electoral cycles in established systems are less likely to be characterized by extensive political mobilization. Conflicts among groups will not be posed in stark, zero-sum terms. Political leaders will of course be concerned with public support, but they will not be subject to fundamental uncertainty regarding their tenure. Since time horizons will be longer, political leaders can capitalize on "honeymoon" periods to undertake reform initiatives with short-term costs that can be expected to yield longer-term gains. Finally, there is likely to be greater continuity within the bureaucracy and in decisionmaking structures. Governments operating under these circumstances can better afford to accept the political risks of economic stabilization.

Regime Type and Adjustment: Some Empirical Evidence

Comparisons of data on fiscal and credit policy from twenty-five Latin American, African, and Asian countries provide the basis for our exploration of these hypotheses.[9] The selection of cases is based in part on the availability of detailed studies of the adjustment process and does not meet the canons of a scientific sample. Nonetheless, most of the major debtors—both continuous democratic regimes and countries undergoing a democratic transition—are included (see Appendix A).

Table 1 provides an overview of the performance of three sets of countries over the first half of the 1980s: those that experienced continuous democratic or authoritarian rule and those that underwent a democratic transition at some point during the period. Such a comparison has important limitations, but it does suggest the broad effects of regime continuity on economic policy.

Two findings are striking. First, the macroeconomic policy stances of the continuous democratic regimes are virtually indistinguishable from those of authoritarian regimes. Second, countries undergoing democratic transitions appeared to pursue more expansionist policies than either established democratic or authoritarian governments. This is particularly clear in the growth of expenditures and in the expansion of central bank credit. Budget deficits were only slightly higher in countries experiencing a transition than under continuous democratic or authoritarian rule, but the differences are not statistically significant. This, however, is in part attributable to the fact that in two transitional cases, the Philippines and Turkey, authoritarian regimes engineered substantial budgetary retrenchment *prior* to the transition to democracy.

Table 2 offers a more disaggregated look at the association between stabilization policies and regime type by examining the implementation of IMF programs. Although the features of these programs vary, virtually all contain provisions on fiscal and monetary policy.[10] The presence of a program is thus an indicator both of macroeconomic problems and of some commitment to correct them. In contrast to Table 1, the unit of analysis is the year in which countries had an IMF program for at least six months.[11] Each such "IMF year" is then classified in terms of the type of regime in power *during that year*. This provides more precise information than the broad categories covering the entire period that are used in Table 1. Table 2 shows the percentage of "IMF program years" in which the countries in each category improved their performance over the previous year. It also shows the percentage of "IMF program years" in which the countries improved their performance compared to the median performance of the sample for that year. This partly corrects for the effect of external shocks influencing the macroeconomic performance of the entire sample.

Several points are noteworthy. First, Table 2 underlines the difficulties that all developing-country governments have in stabilizing. In the aggregate, only 47 per cent of all IMF program years were accompanied by reduced deficits and only 41 per cent by reduced expenditures. In the area of monetary policy there was greater success, with a reduced

Table 1.   Country Policy Performance by Regime Type, 1980–86 (annual change, percentages)

	Democratic Transitions	Continuous Democratic Regimes	Continuous Authoritarian Regimes
Fiscal Deficits/GDP, 1980–86			
Average	−6.7	−5.6	−5.8
Median	−4.6	−3.6	−1.8
	(n = 7)[a]	(n = 11)	(n = 5)
Change in Expenditures/GDP, 1980–85			
Average[b]	55.0	−0.7	0.0
Median	20.4	−2.7	1.1
	(n = 6)	(n = 11)	(n = 6)
Expansion of Central Bank Credit,[c] 1980–85			
Average[d]	58.0	20.6	16.0
Median	64.2	14.9	15.3
	(n = 5)	(n = 11)	(n = 6)

[a]The Philippines is treated as a transitional case in the analysis of budget deficits because of the change of regime in 1986.
[b]One-way analysis of variance $F = 2.625$ (Probability = .10).
[c]Increase in total central bank credit, adjusted for the mean of inflation in the three previous years and current growth. A score of "0" would thus indicate a central bank policy of fully accommodating past inflation and current growth. Bolivia is excluded from the credit sample because of the distortions associated with hyperinflation.
[d]One-way analysis of variance $F = 4.506$ (Probability = .025).

Source: Calculated from data supplied by the World Bank and from International Monetary Fund, *International Financial Statistics*, various issues.

rate of credit expansion in about 62 per cent of IMF program years. The second point of interest is the relative performance of democracies and authoritarian regimes. Again, democratic governments have done as well as authoritarian ones in controlling deficits and credit expansion—though, in contrast to Table 1, democratic governments showed greater difficulties in controlling expenditures.

Finally, though the numbers are small, the data lends support to the hypothesis that democratic political transitions are associated with

Table 2. Performance in Implementing IMF Programs, by Regime Type, 1978–85[a]

	Democratic Transitions	Continuous Democratic Regimes	Continuous Authoritarian Regimes	All Regime Types in All IMF Years
Percentage of IMF Program Years in which Performance Improved Over Previous Year				
Reduced deficit	25.0 (n = 8)	48.7 (n = 39)	50.0 (n = 44)	47.2 (n = 91)
Lowered expenditures/GDP	28.6 (n = 7)	38.2 (n = 34)	46.3 (n = 41)	41.5 (n = 82)
Reduced rate of credit expansion	42.9 (n = 7)	61.3 (n = 34)	61.7 (n = 34)	60.0 (n = 75)
Percentage of IMF Program Years in which Performance Improved Compared to Sample Median for That Year				
Reduced deficit more than median	25.0 (n = 8)	48.7 (n = 39)	50.0 (n = 44)	47.2 (n = 91)
Change in expenditure/GDP less than median	28.6 (n = 7)	35.3 (n = 34)	56.1 (n = 41)	45.1 (n = 82)
Adjusted rate of credit expansion less than median	42.9 (n = 7)	58.1 (n = 34)	58.8 (n = 34)	56.0 (n = 75)

[a]Data for budget deficits, 1978–86; for expenditures, 1978–85; for credit expansion, 1979–85.
Source: Calculated from data supplied by World Bank and from International Monetary Fund, *International Financial Statistics*, various issues.

difficulties in managing macroeconomic policy. With regard to deficits, countries undergoing a transition performed better than the sample median in only 25 per cent of the cases, whereas continuous authoritarian and democratic governments both lowered deficits about half of the time. In transitional years, new democratic governments managed to tighten credit relative to the median in just over 40 per cent of the IMF years, in contrast to almost 60 per cent in the other two categories. Only on fiscal expenditures was there a partial deviation from the general pattern. Although the record of countries in a democratic transition was significantly worse than that of authoritarian regimes, it was only marginally worse than that of established democratic governments.

One possible objection to the effort to correlate regime type with policy choice is that it fails to take into consideration the role of external shocks. In the cases of many developing countries, both fiscal and monetary policy are strongly affected by fluctuations in international commodity prices.[12] Prudence dictates that temporary increases in income associated with commodity booms should be saved, while permanent increases can be spent. When income rises, however, governments are under pressure to assume commitments that cannot be easily abandoned as commodity prices fall. A drop in commodity prices reduces the resources available to governments and increases the level of political conflict. Thus macroeconomic imbalances and political transitions may both be caused by external shocks.

There is no clear evidence that the exogenous shocks faced by countries undergoing democratic transition were generally more severe than those encountered by other types of regimes.[13] More important, not all countries have responded to these pressures in the same way. In Mexico, deficits grew substantially during the oil boom years and experienced an even sharper increase after oil prices dropped in the early 1980s. In contrast, Indonesia's authoritarian regime and Venezuela's established democratic system both kept fiscal deficits under control during the mid-1980s despite fluctuations in oil prices, and Colombia actually managed to cut expenditures during a coffee boom in 1986.

Table 3 provides a closer look at the performance of the countries that experienced democratic transitions during the period 1978–1986. It provides data on the performance in years prior to the transition, during the transition year itself, and in the immediate post-transition period. A base of comparison is provided by the median performance of the sample for the years in question.

Table 3 suggests that, on the whole, governments in countries undergoing democratic transition tended toward expansionist policies—both in comparison to past policy and in comparison with the sample. Nonetheless, the wide variations among the transitional cases in the timing and intensity of their macroeconomic policy problems become apparent. Eight of the ten transitional democracies had higher budget deficits during the transition year than in the period prior to the transition. Argentina, Brazil, and Bolivia, however, experienced especially high deficits during the transition year itself. Surprisingly, five of the ten countries had budget deficits in the transition year that were *lower* than the median for the sample as a whole. In the three years following the transition, however, budget deficits were higher than the median for the sample in six of the eight countries for which there is comparable data, with particular deterioration in Bolivia. In Argentina, the deficit narrowed under the new regime, though it remained well above the median for the sample. In contrast, Uruguay and Ecuador both maintained stable fiscal policy throughout the transition, though Ecuador's performance has since deteriorated badly.

The data on average changes in expenditures also shows both the difficulties that transitional democracies face and the performance variations among them. In the transition year itself, six of the nine governments had increases in expenditures higher than the median, but Argentina, Brazil, and Peru experienced particular surges in government spending. The data for the post-transition period, though less complete, is somewhat more heartening. With the exception of Bolivia, most of the new democracies managed relatively stable shares of government expenditures to gross domestic product (GDP), with slight cuts in expenditures indicated in both Turkey and Thailand.

A comparison of credit policy underscores the differences among authoritarian regimes. Outgoing military governments in Peru, and particularly in Turkey, pursued restrictive monetary policies. In Argentina, Brazil, Bolivia, and Uruguay, in contrast, monetary policy was highly expansionary during the last phase of military rule. These problems carried over into the transition year—except, interestingly, in Uruguay. In the post-transition period, the story is more mixed. Argentina and Thailand slowed their rates of growth of credit expansion. Turkey and the Dominican Republic pursued somewhat looser credit policies. Bolivia experienced hyperinflation, but one that was ultimately tamed under democratic auspices. Not captured in Table 3 are the daunting problems that Argentina, Brazil, Ecuador, and Peru confronted in 1987, 1988, and 1989.

Table 3 also provides data on two recent transitions to authoritarian rule for which there are comparable data: Turkey in 1980 and Ghana in 1983. In both cases, the new military governments acted to control deficits and to slow the expansion of credit. Only in the area of expenditures was policy more expansionist—but only mildly so.

Table 3.   Policy Performance in Democratic and Authoritarian Transition Periods (annual averages[a])

Country/Transition Year	Transition Year and Two Prior Years (sample median[c])		Transition Year (sample median)		Post-Transition Period (sample median[c])	
DEMOCRATIC TRANSITIONS						
Argentina/1983						
Deficits/GDP	−11.3	(−4.5)	−17.2	(−4.1)	−6.6	(−3.9)
Change in						
expenditures/GDP	2.5	(−0.1)	5.4	(−1.4)	0.1	(−0.2)
Credit expansion	277.8	(14.5)	265.0	(22.9)	16.2	(10.0)[d]
Bolivia/1983						
Deficits/GDP	−17.9	(−4.5)	−20.7	(−4.1)	−26.6	(−3.9)
Change in						
expenditures/GDP	8.9	(−0.1)	−7.2	(−1.4)	13.1	(−0.2)
Credit expansion	186.9	(14.5)	133.5	(22.9)	542.1	(10.0)
Brazil/1985						
Deficits/GDP	−6.4	(−4.1)	−11.0	(−3.6)	n.a.	
Change in						
expenditures/GDP	2.6	(−0.6)	8.6	(0.8)	n.a.	
Credit expansion	103.6	(14.3)	205.4	(6.8)	n.a.	
Dominican Rep./78						
Deficits/GDP	−0.9	(−2.8)	−1.5	(−1.9)	−3.6	(−3.4)
Change in						
expenditures/GDP	−0.5	(0.1)	1.4	(0.1)	0	(0.9)
Credit expansion	n.a.		5.9	(10.8)	11.9	(7.6)
Ecuador/1979						
Deficits/GDP	−0.9	(−2.8)	−0.6	(−3.3)	−3.5	(−4.2)
Change in						
expenditures/GDP	−0.7	(0)[d]	−0.5	(−0.1)	1.6	(0.9)
Credit expansion	n.a.		12.3	(7.4)	16.1	(7.6)
Peru/1980						
Deficits/GDP	−0.4	(−2.8)	−2.8	(−3.3)	−5.9	(−4.5)
Change in						
expenditures/GDP	−0.8	(0.4)	5.4	(1.3)	0.7	(−0.1)
Credit expansion	−9.7	(8.3)	−17.0	(6.8)	57.3	(14.5)

[a]The number of cases is too small to permit difference of means test for within-country comparisons.

[b]The post-transition period is defined as the three years following the transition year whenever possible: Comparable data for deficits goes through 1986, but data for expenditures and credit expansion only through 1985. This means that some items for some countries can only be calculated for less than three years. Thus the transition period for Uruguay's budget deficits is data for 1986 only, etc.

Country/Transition Year	Transition Year and Two Prior Years (sample median[c])		Transition Year (sample median)	Post-Transition Period (sample median[c])	
The Philippines/1986					
Deficits/GDP	−1.8	(−3.9)	−5.0 (−3.4)	n.a.	
Change in					
expenditures/GDP	n.a.		n.a.	n.a.	
Credit expansion	n.a.		n.a.	n.a.	
Thailand/1979					
Deficits/GDP	−3.6	(−2.8)	−3.8 (−3.3)	−4.9	(−4.2)
Change in					
expenditures/GDP	0.3	(0)	0.7 (−0.1)	−0.5	(1.0)
Credit expansion	n.a.		27.1 (7.4)	4.4	(9.2)
Turkey/1983					
Deficits/GDP	−2.1	(−4.5)	−2.6 (−4.1)	−4.0	(−3.9)
Change in					
expenditures/GDP	0.1	(−0.1)	0.6 (−1.4)	−1.0	(−0.2)
Credit expansion	−37.1	(14.5)	−28.0 (22.9)	12.3	(10.0)
Uruguay/1985					
Deficits/GDP	−3.8	(−4.1)	−2.2 (−3.6)	−0.6	(−3.4)
Change in					
expenditures/GDP	1.1	(−0.6)	−4.8 (0.8)	n.a.	
Credit expansion	66.7	(14.3)	5.8 (6.8)	n.a.	

AUTHORITARIAN TRANSITIONS

Turkey/1980					
Deficits/GDP	−4.8	(−2.8)	−3.8 (−3.3)	−2.1	(−4.5)
Change in					
expenditures/GDP	−1.9	(0.4)	−1.1 (1.3)	0.1	(−0.1)
Credit expansion	32.6	(8.3)	−39.3 (6.8)	−37.1	(14.5)
Ghana/1983					
Deficits/GDP	−4.9	(−4.5)	−2.7 (−4.1)	−1.3	(−3.9)
Change in					
expenditures/GDP	−2.6	(−0.1)	−3.9 (−1.4)	2.5	(−0.2)
Credit expansion	−8.5	(14.5)	3.4 (22.9)	−16.4	(10.0)

[c]For the pre- and post-transition periods, the numbers in parentheses are means of the sample medians for the three-year period.
[d]Data on expenditures for pre-transition period in Ecuador includes only 1977 and 1978.
Sources: Calculated from International Monetary Fund, *International Financial Statistics,* various issues, and from data provided by the World Bank.

Variations in the Adjustment Experience of New Democracies

The data provides some evidence that systems in democratic transition face particular problems, but it also makes clear that not all face them to the same degree. Thailand and Uruguay have fared better than Peru, Argentina, and Brazil. Why this is so cannot be pinned down with precision, but several factors appear important. These include the economic legacy of the outgoing regime, the degree of institutional continuity between the old regime and the new, the nature and extent of political mobilization during the transition, and the coalitional strategies of the leadership.

The Policy Context and the Economic Legacy of the Outgoing Regime

One hypothesis is that the transition process is less important in explaining variations in performance than the nature of the economic problems that the incoming democratic governments face—including, most obviously, the severity of their debt burdens. These different legacies from the authoritarian period affect economic prospects directly, but we emphasize that they also shape the *politics* of economic policy during the transition period. The efforts of new democratic governments to bring deficits and monetary policy under control while promoting growth are especially complicated by high inflation. A number of Latin American countries undergoing political transitions in the last decade have experienced annual inflation rates of over 100 per cent; these were often coupled with negative economic growth. Argentina, Bolivia, Brazil, and Uruguay inherited high inflation from severely weakened military governments. Mexico, which is experiencing political liberalization, also has had very high inflation in recent years.

In countries with chronically high inflation, governments seek to accommodate social pressures and to reduce the conflict over income shares through indexing. Indexing itself generates inertial inflation, however, complicating the conduct of fiscal and monetary policy. As interest rates on government debt are indexed to past and expected future rates of inflation, interest payments absorb an increasingly larger share of expenditures. Inflation itself becomes a major factor contributing to fiscal deficits. In Mexico, ballooning service costs on government debt undermined the efforts of the administration of President Miguel de la Madrid to keep investment in social programs in line with revenues. When Mexico's budget deficits are corrected for the effect of inflation on interest payments (the "operational budget"), deficits are actually lower in the 1980s than they were in the 1970s; deleting interest payments entirely from budget calculations (the "primary budget") shows that there were actually surpluses during the 1980s. Nonetheless, the full financial deficit continued to escalate during the 1980s, suggesting a process beyond the control of the government.

In the new democracies that faced high inflations, it is less likely that these distortions concealed efforts to close deficits. Rather, high inflation and erratic growth made the distributional and political costs of stabilization through the orthodox means of fiscal and monetary stringency appear particularly formidable. In the mid-1980s, Brazil under President José Sarney and Peru under President Alan García responded to high inflation with "heterodox" policies that included wage and price controls and currency reforms. In contrast to the steps taken in Mexico, neither new democratic government placed a high priority on containing wage pressures, reducing subsidies, or controlling spending, and both experiments ran into difficulties. Argentina's President Raúl Alfonsín, relying less on "popular sector" than on middle-class support, also pursued a heterodox shock policy to manage a high inflation, but placed greater emphasis on negotiating wage restraint and bringing deficits under control. Nonetheless, fiscal policy has continued to be a source of inflationary pressure in Argentina.

New democratic governments in other countries faced different economic and policy legacies that provided greater leeway in formulating policy—both economic and political. The mismanagement of the Philippine economy by the government of Ferdinand Marcos is legendary, but it did succeed in stabilizing the economy prior to its ouster. This allowed the Aquino government to focus on the less controversial task of restoring economic growth. Somewhat larger budget deficits in 1986 were in fact condoned by the IMF and the World Bank. At the same time, since Marcos's interventionist economic policies had been widely discredited by corruption and cronyism, the Aquino government could portray various structural adjustment policies, such as trade liberalization and tax reform, as ways to correct the abuses of the deposed regime.

In the Republic of Korea, stabilization had also been achieved prior to the democratic transition. Incoming President Roh Tae Woo inherited large current account surpluses; and historically high rates of growth had resumed, giving the administration some political leeway. The government refused to intervene to dampen new labor demands, and it capitulated to legislative pressures to raise the government purchase price of rice. On the whole, however, the government took advantage of the surpluses to continue structural reforms such as trade and financial market liberalization. In Brazil, a realistic exchange rate policy, capped by a major devaluation in 1983, also left the incoming Sarney administration with a strong export sector. In contrast to Korea, however, the surpluses were dissipated in expansionist policies.

Political Mobilization, Institutional Capacity, and Continuity

The differences outlined above suggest the importance of politics in understanding economic policy during the transition. New democratic governments vary in the extent of political mobilization that they encounter during the transition and in the relationship between this mobilization and the institutional capacities of government to channel societal demands.[14] In this regard it is useful to distinguish three broad types of democratic transitions based on the depth of popular sector mobilization and the continuity and strength of political institutions.

Political transitions in the first group—Argentina, Uruguay, Peru, and to a lesser extent, Brazil—opened the way for well-organized "popular sector" groups to re-enter the political system. The short-lived transition in Nigeria in the early 1980s offered new opportunities for ethnic politics to resurface. These polities all have long histories of organized labor and a "popular sector"—and, in Nigeria's case, of ethnic-regional organizations with historic ties to political parties. The activities of these organizations had been controlled or repressed under military rule. All have highly skewed distributions of income and wealth.

In these polities, the transition to democracy thus opened the door not only to social-political conflicts over income shares but also to more profound struggles over the shape of the new political order. Important changes occurred in the balance of power among institutional and economic interests competing for the resources of the state. As political leaderships attempted to accommodate strongly conflicting demands, it became difficult to maintain macroeconomic stability. Interestingly, the three experiments with heterodox adjustment strategies—Brazil, Argentina, and Peru—occurred in systems with a high level of popular sector mobilization.

The exception is Uruguay—one of the most successful transitional cases—where the return to constitutionalism restored the two broad-based, centrist parties that had dominated political life prior to the military coup of 1973. This provided an established framework of elite negotiation and accord much like that in more established democratic systems such as those of Colombia, Venezuela, and Costa Rica. Negotiations between the Blanco and Colorado parties led in early 1985 to an economic policy agreement that placed a high priority on controlling budget deficits and inflation, promoting exports, and undertaking structural reforms. The data presented in Table 3 suggests that the administration of President Julio Sanguinetti has operated more or less within these guidelines.

The second group of countries undergoing democratic transition includes Bolivia and Ecuador. As in Peru and Argentina, authoritarian regimes in these countries collapsed in total discredit, with the armed forces deeply divided. Bolivia, Ecuador, and the Dominican Republic have historically had a low level of political institutionalization, how-ever—and the personalism, permeability of the bureaucracy, and insta-bility that marked the old military governments have persisted in vary-ing degrees in their nominally democratic successors. Over the longer term, these governments will probably continue to face problems in for-mulating coherent economic policy. This general institutional weakness has not, however, precluded decisive action in the short run: The concen-tration of decisionmaking authority in the hands of President Victor Paz Estenssoro allowed him to deal quickly and effectively with a hyperin-flation in late 1985; the government of President Leon Febres Cordero in Ecuador initiated wide-ranging reforms following his election in 1984; and President Jorge Blanco managed a briefly successful stabili-zation in the Dominican Republic in 1985.

A third category of transitions consists of those exhibiting a lower level of popular sector mobilization and greater institutional continuity in state-society relations and economic decisionmaking structures. Not coincidentally, these countries also faced less daunting economic prob-lems, and it could be argued that varying economic circumstances rather than political factors were responsible for the nature of policy. It nonetheless appears plausible that political structures had at least an intervening effect on policy choices and outcomes.

Turkey represents perhaps the clearest case of a "democratic" tran-sition engineered from above—by the military. Preparations for return to civilian rule began almost immediately following the military take-over in September 1980. After the coup, the architect of the military's successful economic program, Turgut Özal, was promoted to Deputy Prime Minister. Elections were held in November 1983, but pre-1980 political leaders were banned from participation, parties had to win military approval, and sections of the country remained under martial law. Özal's Motherland Party won a majority in Parliament, providing fundamental policy continuity through the transition.

Democratic transitions in Thailand, Korea, and the Philippines all involved greater degrees of political mobilization and protest than in Turkey—but in institutional and political settings that allowed for sub-stantial continuity of policy. This continuity contributed to their rela-tively stable macroeconomic policies. In Thailand, the new political order ushered in by parliamentary elections in 1979 might better be labeled "semi-democratic."[15] In 1980, General Kriangsak was forced to resign over economic mismanagement in the face of rising protest and pressure from within the military. Another general, Prem Tinsulanond, was elected to replace him by a large majority in both houses. Prem moved to incorporate opposition parties into a broad-based coalition, yet in Thailand's "bureaucratic polity" power continued to reside in the army and the bureaucracy. There were no discontinuities in business-government relations, and technocrats even gained in influence.

In Korea, General Chun Doo-Hwan's handpicked successor, President Roh Tae Woo, was forced to widen the scope of political liberalization and constitutional reform in the face of widespread urban protests in 1986 and 1987. Running against a split opposition, Roh captured the presidency with just over one-third of the popular vote. Although the ruling party subsequently lost control of the National Assembly and has been forced to make a number of political and economic concessions, including some to labor, the executive and the bureaucracy still maintain comparatively tight controls over economic policy.

In the Philippines, the Aquino regime was brought to power by massive middle-class demonstrations against fraudulent elections in February 1986. This "revolution" did not rest on popular sector mobilization, however, and the left made the tactical error of not supporting Aquino's candidacy. Subsequent development planning focused greater attention on rural problems in an effort to counteract an armed insurgency, but President Corazon Aquino also moved quickly to cement ties with those portions of the private sector that had been disadvantaged by the Marcos regime's cronyism. Aquino's economic cabinet was dominated by businessmen turned technocrats. The Central Bank governor, for example, was a conservative banker, and the only holdover from the Marcos period. The reconvening of Congress in 1987 provided new opportunities for economic elites to once again enter the political game. As in Turkey, Thailand, and Korea, fundamental political and institutional continuities restrained political pressures on macroeconomic policy.

Executive Power and Coalitional Strategies

One general characteristic of all of these various transitional situations is that leaders of new democratic governments often enjoy substantial authority, either because of the "honeymoon" effect or because of transitional constitutional provisions that temporarily enlarge their powers. This holds out the possibility for swift and decisive action in the early transition period. In Bolivia, Paz Estenssoro, despite his own populist background, threw the entire authority of the presidency behind the tough austerity measures of 1985 once he was convinced that they were the only way to halt the hyperinflation. The leading trade union organization quickly called for a general strike in opposition to the "new economic policy." As Morales and Sachs have summed up the situation: "After three years of accelerating inflation, and the sense of chaos in early 1985, the government clearly had the upper hand."[16] A temporary state of siege was declared and the strike was quickly broken. In the Philippines, Aquino actually ruled for over a year on an emergency basis that resembled martial law; economic policy was a matter of issuing executive decrees. While Aquino has been criticized for not exploiting this power more fully, it did facilitate a number of economic policy initiatives. Similar periods of executive dominance produced reformist initiatives in Turkey and Thailand.

The concentration of personal presidential power is clearly a two-edged sword, however, since the time horizons of new democratic leaders are likely to be short. The absence of established institutional mechanisms of accountability also raises the possibility of arbitrary behavior. Alan García's nationalization of the banking sector in Peru broke with accords that had been established with business groups and proved fatal to hopes for recovery. In Argentina and Brazil, surprise wage and price packages rested on secrecy and executive power and gained momentary popularity. They eventually unraveled, however, and this might be attributed to least in part to the failure to develop the consultative mechanisms that would have sustained support. Personalism, unpredictability, and at times corruption have also plagued economic policymaking in Ecuador and in the Dominican Republic.

The power of the executive during periods of democratic transition is also partly a result of the fluidity of political coalitions. Political leaders rarely have unconstrained power to determine which social groups will support their governments. In all societies, political alignments are shaped by prior commitments, institutional loyalties, and historic antagonisms, as well as by the policy commitments and appeals of leaders. Nevertheless, incoming democratic leaders may be in a strong position to define the terms of political debate within transitional settings, when very broad anti-authoritarian coalitions are likely to fracture.

The cases under review suggest that *if fiscal and monetary policy stability are viewed as a primary objective,* coalitional strategies that limit mass appeals and dampen expectations are likely to have greater success. Ruling coalitions appealing to the middle class and to business groups are more likely to succeed in attaining these goals than those that seek to appeal to a wider array of social forces. Brazil provides an example. In the effort to build the broadest possible support for a five-year term of office, José Sarney ignored the warnings of many technical advisors and sustained an unviable expansionist policy. In hindsight, Sarney's interests, as well as Brazil's, would have been better served by policies that appealed to a more limited segment of the political spectrum. Alan García's populism in Peru, and the gestures of the administration of the late President José López Portillo in Mexico, provide even more telling examples. The biggest mistake of these leaders was in succumbing to the temptation to use expansionist macroeconomic policy to try to please everyone at the same time.

It is important to raise three caveats to this argument, however. First, fiscal and monetary stability may not be appropriate economic goals in all cases. In the Philippines, a more expansionist economic policy was an appropriate stimulus to growth. Second, the adoption of populist strategies must itself be understood; in settings where a reversion to authoritarian rule looms as a possibility, the economic costs of a populist strategy may appear small when weighed against the perceived gains in consolidating democratic rule. Finally, a more complete explication of the policies of new democracies would have to examine the *external* strategies that states adopt. For some debtors, a more aggressive external stance vis-à-vis creditors may provide the resources to cushion the effects of stabilization at home.

Summary and Recommendations

This study has been structured around three sets of comparisons. First, we suggested that constitutional governments have done as well as authoritarian regimes in managing fiscal and monetary policy during the 1980s. Second, we found that on the whole new democratic regimes had somewhat greater difficulty than more established regimes of either type in sustaining stable macroeconomic policies. Heightened expectations and renewed opportunities for social groups to engage in political activity placed particular pressures on incoming political leaders.

Our third comparison underlined the significant performance differences among countries undergoing democratic transition. High inflation and low growth complicate macroeconomic management and have the *political* effect of intensifying the struggle to defend income shares. High levels of political mobilization, weak institutions for channeling interests, discontinuities in policymaking authority, and populist leadership strategies add to the problems that some new democracies have faced.

These factors are of course not manipulable by outside actors. Nonetheless, our analysis does have a number of implications for the design of programs:

1. Although macroeconomic management may prove ineffective during the initial transition years, domestic support for cautious macroeconomic policies can be built under democratic auspices as a wider range of electoral groups gain experience in governance. Creditors should therefore be willing to provide support—including debt relief—for a gradualist approach to stabilization.

2. Creditors should remain open to policy experimentation. In high-inflation settings, wage and price controls may not only help to break cycles of inertial inflation; they may also ease the struggle for income shares that accompanies rapid price increases and thus ameliorate the political conditions that sustain inflation.

3. In new democracies where inflation has been tamed, the risks of relatively expansionist policies should not be exaggerated. The case of the Philippines suggests that providing additional assistance may help to consolidate democratic transitions.

4. While supporting gradualism and policy experimentation, donors must be alert to the tendency of new democracies to avoid the supporting fiscal and monetary restraints required to make such programs succeed over the longer run. The timing and magnitude of outside support can be important in this regard. It is appropriate to make external assistance conditional on the implementation of policy reforms. It is generally important, however, that assistance and relief be adequate to generate improved economic performance, which is critical in protecting new democratic leaders from populist pressures.

5. In framing adjustment programs that move beyond stabilization, new democratic governments and their external supporters should capitalize on the failure of outgoing governments. Government interventions that were associated with corruption and mismanagement may be easier to dismantle during the transition period than during a setting of "politics as usual." Creditors should therefore be alert to how increased executive autonomy or legitimacy creates "honeymoons" during which structural reforms can be launched.

Notes

Note: The authors wish to thank Susan Collins, Laura Hastings, David Lindauer, Pamela Metz, Joan Nelson, and Jane Sjogren for assistance and comments on earlier drafts. Lauren Burnbauer, Nancy Gilson, Nancy Llach, and Diana Owen assisted in the data analysis. We also thank the participants in seminars sponsored by the Harvard Institute for International Development and the Overseas Development Council.

[1] On the politics of macroeconomic policy in the advanced industrial states, see James Alt and Alec Chrystal, *Political Economics* (Berkeley: University of California Press, 1984); Douglas Hibbs, *The American Political Economy* (Cambridge Mass.: Harvard University Press, 1987).

[2] This is the theme of the World Bank's *World Development Report 1988* (New York: Oxford University Press for the World Bank, 1988).

[3] We define democracy as a government in which (a) leaders are chosen in competitive elections; (b) principles of free speech and assembly are respected by the incumbent authorities and other power contenders; (c) election results are honored without reprisals against the losers; and (d) elected governments are not systematically subject to the broad control or veto of non-elected individuals or outside institutions, whether the military, a monarchy, or the bureaucracy. Authoritarian regimes, in contrast, are those that do not permit open political competition, restrict access to the political process in various ways, and systematically restrict the space allowed to oppositional or interest group activity. See Myron Weiner, "Empirical Democratic Theory," in Myron Weiner and Ergun Ozbuan, eds., *Competitive Elections in Developing Countries* (Durham, N.C.: Duke University Press, 1987); Guillermo O'Donnell and Philippe C. Schmitter, "Tentative Conclusions about Uncertain Democracies," in O'Donnell, Schmitter, and Laurence Whitehead, eds., *Transitions from Authoritarian Rule* (Baltimore, Md.: The Johns Hopkins University Press, 1986).

[4] Karen Remmer, "The Politics of Economic Stabilization: IMF Standby Programs in Latin America, 1954–1984," *Comparative Politics* (October 1986).

[5] Stephan Haggard, "The Politics of Adjustment: Lessons from the IMF's Extended Fund Facility," in Miles Kahler, ed., *The Politics of International Debt* (Ithaca, N.Y.: Cornell University Press, 1986). See also Joan Nelson, "The Politics of Stabilization," in Richard E. Feinberg and Valeriana Kallab, eds., *Adjustment Crisis in the Third World* (New Brunswick, N.J.: Transaction Books in cooperation with the Overseas Development Council, 1984).

[6] Barry Ames, *Political Survival* (Berkeley: University of California Press, 1987), p. 33.

[7] Stephan Haggard and Robert Kaufman, "The Politics of Stabilization and Structural Adjustment," in Jeffrey Sachs, ed., *Developing Country Debt and Economic Performance: The International Financial System* (Chicago: University of Chicago Press, 1989), pp. 235–39.

[8] Below, we compare performance in the transition year itself, and the three years that follow. A number of cases—the Dominican Republic, Ecuador, and Thailand—experienced democratic transitions in the late 1970s; whether they are considered transitional or established depends on the period under review.

[9] See also Robert Kaufman and Barbara Stallings, "Debt and Democracy in the 1980s: The Latin American Experience," in Kaufman and Stallings, eds., *Debt and Democracy in Latin America* (Boulder, Colo.: Westview Press, 1989).

[10] On the content of IMF programs, see Fiscal Affairs Department, International Monetary Fund, *Fund-Supported Programs, Fiscal Policy, and Income Distribution*, IMF Occasional Paper No. 46 (Washington, D.C., September 1986).

[11] See Remmer, "The Politics of Economic Stabilization," op. cit.

[12] See World Bank, *World Development Report 1988*, op. cit., pp. 86–91.

[13] For evidence on this point, see Bela Balassa and F. Desmond McCarthy, "Adjustment Policies in Developing Countries, 1979–1983," World Bank Staff Working Paper No. 675 (Washington, D.C.: The World Bank, 1984).

[14] This formulation is drawn from Samuel Huntington, *Political Order in Changing Societies* (New Haven, Conn.: Yale University Press, 1968).

[15] See Chai-Anana Samudavija, "Thailand: A Stable Semi-Democracy," in Larry Diamond, Juan J. Linz, and Seymour Martin Lipset, *Democracy in Developing Countries: Asia* (Boulder, Colo.: Lynne Rienner Publishers, 1989).

[16] Juan Antonio Morales and Jeffrey D. Sachs, "Bolivia's Economic Crisis," in Sachs, ed., *Developing Country Debt and the World Economy* (Chicago: University of Chicago Press, 1988), p. 74.

Appendix A: Classification of Countries by Regime Type, 1978–86

Democratic Transitions[a]	Continuous Democratic Regimes	Continuous Authoritarian Regimes
Argentina	Colombia	Chile
Bolivia	Costa Rica	Indonesia
Brazil	India	Korea, Republic of
Dominican Republic	Jamaica	Mexico
Ecuador	Malaysia	Zambia
Ghana[a]	Papua New Guinea	
Nigeria[a]	Sri Lanka	
Peru	Venezuela	
Philippines		
Thailand		
Turkey[a]		
Uruguay		

[a]Countries that experienced a transition to democratic rule between 1978 and 1986. Three of these countries experienced transitions to authoritarian rule during the period: Ghana and Nigeria in 1983, and Turkey in 1980. In the text tables, data for the "Democratic Transition" category is based on varying subsets of this list depending on the particular year(s) in question.

Source: Authors' classification.

Chapter 3

Democratization and Disinflation: A Comparative Approach

Laurence Whitehead

This chapter concerns two critical issues on which a great deal of recent scholarly attention has been lavished: How do fragile new democracies (sometimes) become consolidated? And how can triple-digit inflation (sometimes) be tamed? In most of Latin America, these are of course burning issues not just for social scientists, or even for those in positions of power and responsibility, but for the emerging citizenry as a whole.

From a practical standpoint, economic policymakers and economic agents need to judge whether the processes of democratic transition and consolidation are likely to support, impede, or prohibit economic stabilization; but the intellectual rationale for such judgments is often extremely shaky. To business analysts, non-economic considerations may appear to intrude in an arbitrary and unpredictable manner on the orderly processes of coordination through the market. Democratic politicians are similarly called upon to make practical judgments about how far the "technically rational" measures recommended by those responsible for sound management of the economy are likely to assist, hamper, or destroy the prospects of regime consolidation. From their standpoint, the advice of technocrats is liable to seem unwelcome and almost impossible to challenge, but also very difficult to implement by consensual means.

This chapter sets out in summary form one view of the logic of democratic consolidation, and one view of the issues involved in inflation control. Both goals are important, and both interact with each other. One way to explore these interactions is to consider the role of stabilizing expectations as a possible analytical link between the two processes.

The Logic of Democratic Consolidation

The transition from authoritarian rule necessarily involves a period of high political uncertainty. The length of this interlude and the scale of the accompanying uncertainties vary markedly from case to case. If the democratization remains on track, however, in due course the many uncertainties of the transition period are progressively diminished as the new assumptions and procedures become better known and understood as well as more widely accepted. The new democratic regime will become *institutionalized,* its framework of open and competitive political expression will become *internalized,* and thus in large measure the preceding uncertainties and insecurities will be overcome. Such a process may well take a decade or more.

When a democratization process advances from end-transition to full consolidation, there is (1) a widening of the range of political actors who assume democratic conduct on the part of their adversaries; (2) a deepening of the commitment of most actors to the mutually negotiated democratic framework (i.e., they increasingly take a *principled* rather than an *instrumental* approach to the observance of this framework); and thus (3) an interactive sequence akin to a round of tariff cuts, or arms reduction in international relations, whereby all participants in the democratic game withdraw some of the barriers to enhanced trust and cooperation with their rivals. By these means, political actors learn to change their perceptions of themselves, their significant potential opponents, and the system as a whole. Their expectations of the democratic system become stabilized.

This perspective on democratic consolidation directs attention toward *processes* of political interaction but away from the substantive *policies* that need to be adopted. The evidence suggests that a surprisingly wide range of policy choices may be compatible with democratic consolidation, provided that agreed procedures are observed in making such choices.

Nevertheless, there is *some* limit to the speed and scale of social redistribution compatible with democratic consolidation. Those who wish to stabilize a fragile democracy will at least initially be obliged to offer some guarantees to the privileged classes inherited from the authoritarian period. Put more crudely, it will be necessary to "purchase the allegiance" of the bourgeoisie. How high a price it is necessary to pay may be a question of fine judgment, but the principle is clear. Those who insist on using the transition to press for unrestrained redistribution are not promoting stable democratization. Consciously or not, they are a destablizing factor.

Is there also a limit on the other side—some minimal redistribution or social reform without which the incipient democracy will suffer, having failed to distance itself in any way from the inequities of the authoritarian period? In principle there should be, but in practice it may take very little in material rewards to purchase the allegiance of the lower classes. Liberals would say this is because political freedom is as much an aspiration of the poor as of the rich. Radicals might explain the asymmetry by pointing to the high expectations and strong capacity for organization of the bourgeoisie compared to that of the masses. Latin American societies are far from uniform in this respect, however. Moreover, the distribution of social power may shift quite markedly in the course of democratization. Thus the *timing* of any shift toward redistributive policies may be more critical than its *scale* in determining the course of regime consolidation.

In a well-consolidated democracy, a broad array of social interests and of political tendencies will be free to articulate their policy positions and to compete responsibly for public office. This is in sharp contrast to the exclusions of the authoritarian period and to the uncertainties and insecurities of the first phase of democracy. It may involve a substantial shift in the distribution of social power if, for example, mass membership political parties, trade unions, and popular organizations achieve electoral influence where formerly public office was monopolized by narrow privileged elites. (This is a possible rather than a necessary outcome of full democratization, however—the old elites may themselves achieve electoral success.)

Overambitious policies of redistribution adopted too early in the process of democratization are unlikely to be well worked out—or to rest on a stable consensus. Politically effective and socially durable redistribution may involve shifts in public spending or in regional or sectoral priorities rather than direct shifts from profits to wages. Such redistributive measures may be more successful and may contribute more to the consolidation of democracy if they are phased in over time as the balance of social power shifts.

Inflation Control

If democratic consolidation takes a variety of forms (from Switzerland to Costa Rica, from Greece to Botswana), the control of inflation embraces a considerably wider range of distinct possibilities. One variant would be national adherence to some system of restraints such as the gold standard, Bretton Woods, or the European Monetary System. Another would be the adoption of a series of non-market internal disciplines effectively repressing inflation (as in revolutionary Cuba). Or the opposite political formula might also be used to sustain price stability—i.e., a traditional authoritarian and exclusionary form of capitalism that could compel the lower classes unresistingly to absorb all price shocks (as in Guatemala under Jorge Ubico). A third possibility would be simply to dispense with monetary sovereignty, allowing the dollar to substitute for any national currency (Panama). But none of these archetypal and dominating forms of inflation control are realistic options for the fragile democracies of contemporary South America. Indeed, ever since the first oil price shock of 1973, inflation in Latin America as a whole has progressively risen above the levels prevailing in the rich industrial countries—with the worst acceleration occurring in the most recent subperiod (see Table 1).

In such a setting, the control of inflation becomes a very relative concept. Instead of regarding price stability as an overriding economic policy objective, Latin American policymakers have generally viewed it as one desideratum among many, and they have been willing to tolerate double- or even triple-digit inflation rates rather than to make the requisite sacrifices in other areas to eliminate inflation.

The record of the eight Latin American republics that currently hold periodic, free, competitive elections discloses only two years of single-digit inflation over the past decade—Venezuela in 1978 and 1983

Table 1.   Consumer Price Inflation

	Percentage Increase Over Preceding Year				
	1971-73	1974-78	1979-82	1983-85	1986-88
Industrial Countries	5→9	13→7	9→8	5→4	2→4
Western Hemisphere Developing Countries[a]	16→31	38→41	47→73	118→161	83→>300[b]

[a]Excludes Venezuela until 1980.
[b]The final figure, >300 per cent, is a rough estimate based on U.N. Economic Commission for Latin America and the Caribbean (ECLAC), "Preliminary Overview of the Latin American Economy," *Notas sobre la Economía y el Desarrollo,* No. 470/471 (Santiago, Chile: December 1988), Table 5, p. 17, which estimates regional consumer price inflation from December to December at 64.5 per cent in 1986; 198.9 per cent in 1987; and 472.8 per cent in 1988 (November to November).

Source: Simplified from International Monetary Fund, *International Financial Statistics* (Washington, D.C.: IMF), various issues.

(see Table 2). There are also only two years of four- and five-digit inflation—Bolivia in 1984 and 1985 (although Peru subsequently qualified in 1988).

Well-trained economists confronted by this discouraging panorama are apt to recommend drastic corrective action to bring the region's intractable experience back into harmony with their theoretical notions and a well-functioning price system as speedily as possible. But more seasoned policymakers and more experienced democratic politicians have learned the hard way that there are no miracle cures. Even if it is possible to achieve very drastic temporary reductions in measured inflation, no official commitment to permanent price stability has proven durable or credible over the past twenty years. If expectations of a progressively more stable price level are to take hold, policymakers will have to set themselves initial targets that are realistic and sustainable. This rules out zero inflation.

Thus the form of inflation control that is relevant for this chapter involves:

(1) Resisting policies that would lead to the cumulative acceleration of inflation;

(2) Designing measures that allow a relatively normal functioning of the economy at fairly high but stable levels of inflation; and

(3) Where such measures prove inadequate, introducing policies to force down the underlying rate of price increase—without, however, expecting to achieve absolute price stability.

All three elements of inflation control involve a very large degree of discretionary regulation ("fine tuning") by the country's economic managers. At frequent (but unpredictable) intervals, they must decide which of the three types of policy applies in current circumstances. Then they must decide the precise steps to be taken, the combination of instruments to be used, and the timetable to be followed. Finally, they must attempt to reconcile the latest phase of inflation management with other critical aspects of economic policymaking such as debt management, export promotion, regional balance, and employment policies.

This is the staple fare of South America's economic managers, and it requires a combination of technical sophistication, mental agility, stamina, managerial skill, and pure luck that few ordinary mortals possess. They serve at the apex of extremely cumbersome and unreliable administrative machines, they work with statistics of questionable accuracy, and they are subject to intense pressures of various kinds from the social sectors most affected by their policy decisions. All this applies to even the most insulated technocrats working within the most secure of authoritarian regimes. If one adds the constraints characteristic of

Table 2. Inflation and Democratization in Eleven Countries

	Percentage Increase Over Preceding Year										
	1978	1979	1980	1981	1982	1983	1984	1985	1986	1987	1988
Argentina	176	160	101	105	165	344	627	672	90	131	300+
Bolivia	10	20	47	32	124	276	1,281	11,750	276	15	21
Brazil	39	53	83	106	98	142	197	227	145	230	800
Colombia (D)	18	25	27	28	25	20	16	24	19	23	28
Costa Rica (D)	6	9	18	37	90	33	12	15	12	17	23
Dominican Rep.	4	9	17	8	8	5	27	38	10	25	50+
Ecuador	12	10	13	13	16	48	31	28	23	30	80+
Jamaica (D)	35	29	27	13	7	12	28	26	15	7	8
Peru	58	67	59	75	64	111	110	163	78	86	1,300+
Uruguay	45	67	64	34	19	49	55	72	76	64	60+
Venezuela (D)	7	12	22	16	10	6	12	11	12	28	31

Note: _____ designates approximate date of democratic transition; _____ designates approximate date of democratic breakdown. (D) designates countries with democratic government throughout period.

Sources: Simplified from International Monetary Fund, *International Financial Statistics* (Washington, D.C.: IMF), various issues; and U.N. Economic Commission for Latin America and the Caribbean (ECLAC), "Preliminary Overview of the Latin American Economy," *Notas sobre la Economía y el Desarrollo*, No. 470/471 (Santiago, Chile: December 1988), Table 5, p. 17.

constitutional democracy—the need to win support from ill-informed parliaments and party assemblies, the need to take into account the electoral repercussions of particular decisions, the need to compensate losers, and above all, the need patiently to explain, defend, and justify every decision, rather than merely to decree it—the obstacles to effective and sustained inflation control seem truly formidable. It becomes easy enough to understand the periods of inflationary acceleration shown schematically in Table 1, but harder to explain why, despite everything, a degree of inflation control is nevertheless achieved in about half of the region's democracies.

In fact, as Table 2 indicates, even during the debt-ridden 1980s a surprising range of democratic governments *have* reduced inflationary expectations in their countries. Thoroughgoing price stability seems generally unattainable but hyper-inflationary breakdown is also quite avoidable. This indicates that in most countries most economic agents still expect that the authorities can act effectively to avert a complete monetary collapse, even though they cannot credibly pursue price stability. (Similarly, most political actors combine fairly high confidence in the capacity of the new constitutional regimes to survive, with scant faith in their ability to deliver good government.) The path to stabilizing expectations is in principle the same in the economic sphere as in the political sphere. It is therefore essential for the authorities invariably and immediately to shore up the modest positive expectations that persist (i.e., that both hyper-inflation and political regression will be vigilantly combatted). Only with great patience and stamina, however, is it at all likely that entrenched negative expectations (about the endemic character of both economic and political instability) gradually will be unlearned. At best, this second process can only be gradual, tentative, and incremental.

Does Democracy Impede Disinflation?

The most one might claim on the basis of the evidence in Table 2 is that the transition to democracy might give rise to a temporary upsurge in inflation. It would not be possible to assert that democracies in the process of consolidation have a substantially worse record on inflation control than their authoritarian predecessors. The record of long-standing democracies seems appreciably better than that of countries subject to regime change. Some relatively consolidated democracies (Costa Rica, Jamaica, and Venezuela) have proven relatively successful at implementing disinflation policies, and one very fragile new democracy (Bolivia) has achieved the most remarkable turnaround from hyper-inflation to virtual price stability.

This evidence is useful, as far as it goes. But to carry the argument any further, what is needed is an interpretation of how the political and economic variables may interact.

Democratization and Disinflation: The Interactions

Central to the idea of democratic consolidation is the development of a minimum of trust between rival political tendencies, and competing social sectors, where distrust and imposition had been the norm. Central to the process of inflation control in contemporary South America is the extensive use of discretionary power by the national economic authorities. This power involves managing, regulating, and not infrequently shocking private economic agents whose pursuit of self-interest might otherwise lead to uncontrollable inflation.

Whatever its initial history, once any particular inflation has become embedded at the two- or three-digit levels, it becomes an interactive process in which economic managers will appear to many as part-cause rather than all-solution. In short, the style of inflation management required in contemporary South America often seems to involve the sudden arbitrary use of public power by policymakers who are themselves partly responsible for the problems they aim to rectify, and who may act with little consultation or even explanation. It is not a style likely to promote the growth of trust, and for this reason it appears *prima facie* inimical to the consolidation of democracy. Indeed mismanagement or abuse of the great powers entrusted to those responsible for inflation control can cripple the process of democratic consolidation. But equally well, an effective, responsible, and accountable use of these powers would make a major contribution to the growth of trust in the new democratic regime. There are examples of positive and mutually reinforcing interactions as well as of spirals of conflict and demoralization.

The example of democratic Spain provides a model that many Latin Americans view as relatively accessible and relevant to their predicament. Although the circumstances were not the same as in contemporary Latin America, not all the differences were in Spain's favor. When the transition to democracy began in the mid-1970s, Spain had reached a higher level of economic development than the Latin American republics, and inflation was less entrenched. Moreover, the prospect of full political and economic integration into the low-inflation democratic European Community was a great asset compared to the "malign neglect" that seems to have characterized Latin America's international position in the 1980s. But the Franco dictatorship had suppressed political conflicts that were more irreconcilable than the Latin American norm, and the degree and duration of the repression had been worse.

Consequently the task of reestablishing trust and cooperation among Spain's newly emerging political forces seemed at least as formidable as in most of the new Latin American democracies, and the dangers of inexperienced government and of destabilizing lurches in economic policy were thought to be considerable. In the event, however, Spain's new democratic regime rapidly proved capable of conciliating nearly all the political conflicts that had contributed to the Civil War (not just between left and right but also between regions and language groups), as well as of domesticating the armed forces, and of permitting unimpeded alternation in office between parties of radically different ideological provenance. All this was combined with remarkable success on the inflation front—with Spain already converging toward the European norm of low single-digit inflation and an open economy.

The Spanish example does not provide a simple recipe that can be mechanically transferred to the fragile and inflation-prone democracies of Latin America, but it does offer encouragement that, in some circumstances, the processes of democratization and disinflation can be mutually reinforcing. For example, when a new democratic regime manages to weather the strain of the first electorally mandated alternation of government, this success not only reassures the citizenry that the political order is becoming more secure; it can also reassure economic agents that electoral change need not signify too drastic a break in economic policy continuity. Similarly, when a democratic government wins the support of organized interests for its stabilization strategy (or at least circumvents their resistance), this success not only boosts economic confidence but also reinforces the stability of the democratic regime. Thus both political and economic expectations can be conditioned by a single process, even though the two types respond to analytically distinctive logic.

At a general level, we can clarify these connections in two ways: by distinguishing between different subtypes of democratization and of disinflation; and by considering alternative patterns of sequencing. Schematically, we may consider the following alternatives: democratization through "pact" or "rupture"; disinflation based on "orthodoxy" or "heterodoxy"; and the political economy of "gradualism" or "shock."

Various types of social pact have played an important role in the establishment and consolidation of new democracies. Such pacts may be informal understandings or legally binding commitments; they may be confined to agreement on the processes of decisionmaking or may include guarantees on substantive issues; they may be time-limited or of indefinite duration. Whenever democratization is negotiated by means of such a pact, the owners of private capital are always directly or indirectly party to the negotiations. Even when such pacts are informal, time-limited, and mainly concerned with the processes of decisionmaking rather than the resolution of substantive policy questions, the need to provide at least a modicum of reassurance or guarantees to the property-owning classes is always a prominent concern for the pact-makers. Directly alienating the business community would jeopardize a democratic transition at its most delicate moment and would impede the processes of social reconciliation (the growth of trust) that provide the underlying aim of any "pacted" democratization. Reassurance to property owners can take many forms, but a virtually essential ingredient is that their representatives should have easy access to, and confidence in, the economic policymakers. Pacted democratizations are thus constitutionally biased against either radically heterodox or drastically shock strategies of disinflation. They lead more naturally to gradualist, incremental, consultative, and relatively orthodox forms of inflation management and control.

The experiences of Colombia, Venezuela, Ecuador, the Dominican Republic, and Uruguay seem consistent with this interpretation. Brazil and Peru are more difficult to accommodate within this framework—perhaps because in the first case the pact-making process was disrupted by the untimely death of Tancredo Neves, and in the second, the failure of the administration of Fernando Belaúnde and the subsequent election of Alan García undermined the foundational pact before it had become entrenched.

If we disregard cases of external imposition, the main alternative to pacted democratization is "democratic rupture," as in Argentina and Bolivia in 1982. These are also the best two examples of how a democratic transition can lead to a temporary (i.e., two- or three-year) relaxation—or collapse—of the normal mechanisms of inflation control, followed by drastic shock treatment. In a case of democratic rupture, the property owners will not be entitled to the same guarantees or the same easy access to economic policymakers as in a pacted transition. Favored under the previous authoritarian regime, they will have contributed little, if at all, to its demise. In any case, the manner of the demise will have involved confrontation, humiliation, and rout, none of which inspire business confidence or offer much space for intra-elite mediation.

In other words, the messy necessities of democratic rupture are likely—at least temporarily—to disrupt routine economic policymaking as well as to set back the task of reconciliation, which this chapter defines as the essence of long-term democratic consolidation. Just as rupture was not an optimal route out of authoritarian rule, so too the shock treatments of 1985 (heterodox for Argentina, orthodox for Bolivia) were not optimal strategies of inflation control. But in both countries they were the only routes available. What *must* be recognized, however, is that if the long-run goal is democratic consolidation as defined in this chapter, such episodes of rupture and shock constitute notable obstacles to the eventual restoration of trust and social cooperation.

Although "shock treatment" of inflation may sometimes be unavoidable, it is not conducive to democratic consolidation—certainly not if it has to be used repeatedly and unpredictably. (Similarly, an attempted coup may be unavoidable along the road to democratization—and need not necessarily represent a lasting setback—but a *succession* of military revolts becomes progressively more damaging.) This brings us back to the point that both democratic consolidation and disinflation are protracted processes best evaluated over a period of decades, rather than just years or months. In principle, therefore, we should consider whether a certain order or sequence would improve the chances of harmonizing and stabilizing both processes, or whether, on the other hand, there are other sequences that would be fatal to the prospects for success on one count or the other.

Only a very schematic treatment of this issue is possible at this level of generality. It has already been suggested that in transition by rupture, a two- or three-year interval of poor inflation control may be unavoidable while the new regime devotes its energies to resolving the questions of political order that were not settled by prior negotiation or pact. By contrast, pacted transitions may make inflation control relatively easy to maintain in the first period, although economic discipline may relax in the second or third term as voters become more confident that the parties making the highest bids for their support will be allowed to take office if they win. (Democratic Greece first cautiously elected a conservative government, but subsequently opted for Andreas Papandreou and his center-left party PASOK; democratic Peru first clung to Fernando Belaúnde before taking a gamble with Alan García; and in Argentina the Peronists are still waiting their turn.)

In short, as a democracy becomes more secure, the electorate may become more willing to take a few economic risks. Conversely, as democratic politicians acquire more experience of the problems of economic management and become more convinced that they will be held *politically* accountable for the results of their stewardship in office, they become more cautious/realistic/responsible about their electoral promises. The evidence from Latin America's most durable democracies suggests that, over the long run, the second of these trends often outweighs the first. For at least the first generation of voters and their elected representatives, however, the macroeconomic learning curve must not be too flat.

Which sequences of inflation control policy might be expected to accelerate, or impede, this learning process? The most dramatic example of a learning (or over-learning) process occurred in Bolivia after

1982. Hernán Siles and his supporters learned the enormous political (and electoral) cost of abandoning any serious attempt to control inflation. In the light of that experience, Victor Paz Estenssoro veered to the other extreme, putting the restoration of price stability above all other objectives.

It might be argued that it was not politically possible to adopt realistic policies of inflation control during the first phase of democratization. However that may be, all concerned eventually learned the lesson that, in the absence of such policies, both the economic and the political costs of accelerating inflation soar to intolerable levels. Soon any trade-off whatsoever ceases between inflation and redistribution, or inflation and the garnering of electoral support.

The other relatively clear-cut example of a learning process is to discount apparently costless heterodox solutions. There are no miracle cures for inertial inflation, as the electorate of Brazil discovered immediately after the congressional elections of November 1986. Brazil's fragile and incipient democracy was not well served by the policy of pretending that inflation could be painlessly eliminated by a package of mysterious technical devices that required no effort of fiscal discipline or self-restraint by consumers. An unaccountable federal executive dreamed up these measures behind the backs of the emerging political and social groupings and decreed them without consultation.

Because most sequencing choices fall somewhere between these extremes, they fail to yield such clear-cut lessons. For example, in Argentina, Raúl Alfonsín has had to decide how much priority to give to his anti-inflation objectives relative to other, equally pressing goals such as reestablishing civilian control over the military, attracting international assistance to alleviate the debt problem, and maintaining a strong electoral appeal. Trying to keep these various spheres of policy isolated from each other in their separate compartments would have been useless, for they inherently overlap and interact. Thus the size of the defense budget critically affects the campaign for restoring civilian control over the armed forces; it also constrains debt management, and the prospects for inflation control.

Raúl Alfonsín first gave priority to his more strictly political objectives, and his administration neglected inflation control. Initially this might have been a justifiable strategy—given the urgency of the other problems he faced. Until inflation accelerated markedly, the social climate would not be right for the introduction of a counter-inflation strategy such as the July 1985 Austral Plan. Even if we classify this neglect of inflation as a conscious policy choice and accept these retrospective justifications (a more favorable view than many analysts would take), this first timing decision set in train a further sequence of events that would require successive fine judgments of timing and emphasis.

In early 1986, Alfonsín failed to give his economic team the strong backing they would have needed to extend the life of their plan. Other political objectives received higher priority, and the stabilization plan broke down more completely than it might have done otherwise, leaving the Alfonsín administration in 1987 with less room to maneuver on economic management issues than it had hoped. It therefore decided to give priority to correcting economic imbalances before the September 1987 congressional elections. (Here we find the opposite choice to the Brazilian strategy of delaying all corrective meaures until after the November 1986 elections.) As a result of *this* decision, the Radicals suffered an unexpectedly sharp electoral setback, which in turn undermined their ability to control inflation in 1988, and so helped to deprive them of a further term of office in 1989.

This Argentine example (though stylized and incomplete) has been given in some detail to illustrate the complexity of sequencing decisions aimed simultaneously at strengthening democracy and reducing price instability. Even with the benefit of hindsight, the precise lessons to be drawn remain open to dispute. Whether or not a "right" or a "wrong" sequence of decisions can be identified in such cases, any harassed policymaker will justly point out that, one way or another, a sequence must be chosen and lived with.

Standing back a little from the detail of these dilemmas, it needs to be stressed that, in the long run, a history of continuous failure to stabilize or reduce inflation generates such cynicism and such a range of defense mechanisms that the policy alternatives can become increasingly stark and unpleasant. Over time, the process of democratic consolidation involves the production of mechanisms for consultation and decisionmaking that embroil a wide range of political actors in a common project. But over time, laxity in inflation control reduces the scope for gradualist, incremental, and negotiated economic policies—leaving little alternative to confrontation and imposition. Therefore, in the long run, a major precondition for successful democratic consolidation is that there be no cumulative laxity in inflation control but rather a progressive reinforcement of the disciplines underpinning relative price stability. In short, both democratic consolidation and progress against inflation rest on a common foundation: the reinforcement of stabilizing expectations.

Conclusions

This chapter does not pretend to offer a reliable general formula for delivering the required results. If it were so easy, the skilled, dedicated, and experienced policymakers who have been trying to tackle this problem in Argentina would have achieved much better results, and the

International Monetary Fund would be widely welcomed for its helpful prescriptions instead of feared for its painful and frequently ineffective remedies. Some ways of thinking about the processes of democratization and disinflation, and their possible interactions, have been suggested to provide some perspective to policymakers who are frequently overwhelmed by the pressures of each crisis. Beyond immediate tactical considerations, strategic objectives that may take a decade or more to achieve must be kept in view. Economic and political objectives should not be separated into watertight compartments, since a single policy stance can act powerfully in both areas, each of which may interact strongly with the other. Economic theorists may be impatient with the untidiness, irrationality, and waste that characterize endemic inflation, but they will not produce successful policy by trying to impose a system that is at variance with the deeply entrenched expectations of all real economic agents. Thus, for example, to tolerate double-digit inflation might be a disastrous strategy in a society accustomed to price stability, but it could represent a very considerable success (and the most credible goal to aim for) in a society that has adjusted to the three-digit level. Similarly, to demand Scandinavian democratic purity from a fragile Latin American regime could be unrealistic and counterproductive. Progress toward democratization has to be assessed within the context of a nation's own history.

Such relativism and respect for context must of course be combined with a commitment to some basic standards. In this endeavor, it helps to view both democratization and disinflation as long-term processes that can be approached through a variety of paths but with pre-specified outcomes.

This perspective on the problem should be considered not just by Latin American policymakers but also by those in the international community who wish to support the consolidation of stable and open democracies in the Western Hemisphere. International attitudes toward Southern Europe and Latin America contrast markedly in this respect. For thirty years the European Community has made clear the eventual outcome it was seeking to promote in authoritarian Southern Europe and the long-term incentives it was willing to offer (full and irreversible Community membership, with long-term financial assistance to ease the transition to liberal capitalist democracy). Although the eventual objective was quite precise, the timing and route to its achievement were not specified from outside. Instead it was left to the peoples of Greece, Portugal, and Spain to work out their own paths to democratization-with-market stability with only limited and unobtrusive external conditionality.

The international community, in contrast, seems to have no comparably firm image of Latin America's future—let alone how such long-term goals might be promoted. Moreover, the external influences that are brought to bear on Latin America's fragile democracies are generally fragmented and poorly coordinated (often even incoherent), short-term, erratic, and intrusive. (Consider the Reagan administration's policies toward Argentina, for example, or IMF/World Bank relations with democratic Brazil.) Admittedly the erratic policies of these external actors may merely respond to the instabilities generated from within each of the Latin American republics.

Whatever the cause, the overall result is all too clear. Frequently such exernal influences (however well-intentioned) contribute to the destabilization of expectations rather than to their harmonization. The implications for Western policymakers are also clear. If they wish to contribute more effectively to long-run democratization and disinflation in Latin America, they need to introduce a steady, durable, and multilateral framework of incentives. They should avoid backing any particular local faction against its rivals, and they should strengthen the autonomy of internal institutions rather than seek to penetrate and manipulate them. The European precedent indicates that such a shift in the pattern of external influence could have a substantial positive effect over the long run.

Chapter 4

The Politics of Pro-Poor Adjustment

Joan M. Nelson

When the debt crisis first broke, the prevailing assumption was that regaining balance and resuming growth might demand harsh measures, but could be accomplished fairly rapidly. Some governments immediately combined adjustment measures with steps to protect the poor, but the issue was not high on the international agenda. As the full scope and depth of the crisis emerged, its social costs also became more obvious. UNICEF's pair of volumes on *Adjustment with a Human Face* focused and legitimized concerns that had been mounting in many quarters.

At the same time, in much of the developing world, adjustment efforts face rising popular political resistance, often labeled "adjustment fatigue." The growing list of governments in countries newly turning or returning to democracy must deal with acute tensions between consolidating fragile political openings and pursuing realistic economic policies. Many argue that more pro-poor adjustment programs might improve political sustainability as well as reduce suffering. But pro-poor measures, especially those going beyond short-term relief, pose political difficulties of their own.

This paper first considers the factors shaping the commitment of governments to pro-poor policies. It then examines the politics of different types of pro-poor measures. The final section considers whether pro-poor measures would ease the political pressures facing many governments.

Each of these questions is affected by how "the poor" are defined.

Different agencies and actors often have in mind quite different concepts of the poor.

- Many humanitarian organizations give highest priority to reaching "the poorest of the poor." Michael Lipton provides a working definition of the ultra-poor as those who spend virtually all of their incomes on food yet cannot afford adequate caloric intake.[1] The ultra-poor differ systematically from the poor and need special programs. The fragmentary data available suggest that the ultra-poor may comprise the poorest 10–20 per cent in low-income African and South Asian nations and a smaller proportion in somewhat better off countries.

- UNICEF, in accord with its mandate, is concerned with an overlapping but different category: the vulnerable poor—above all young children and pregnant women—for whom even fairly short periods of severe hardship threaten permanent physical and mental damage. (That standard seems narrower then "the ultra poor," but in poor countries and hard times may be much broader.)

- The World Bank, the U.S. Agency for International Development (USAID), and other development agencies usually define "the poor" more broadly. In the late 1970s, the World Bank used the poorest 40 per cent as a rough rule of thumb; in the late 1980s, the bottom 30 per cent is the often-used standard.[2] This category is almost entirely rural. In the poorest countries, many of these people are Lipton's "ultra poor"; elsewhere most are often hungry but not semi-starving.

- Most politicians and political activists in developing countries define "the poor" (or "the popular classes") still more inclusively. Indeed, they usually have in mind less the bottom third than the middle deciles, including the urban poor and near-poor and the rural groups falling in the fourth through seventh deciles of the national income distribution.[3]

Each of these definitions of the poor points toward different designs and costs of pro-poor measures. Each also has quite different political implications, as discussed below.

Political Commitment to Helping the Poor

Political obstacles to pro-poor policies are often viewed simply as a manifestation of selfish vested interests that can be overcome by right-minded and determined leaders. The first volume of UNICEF's *Adjustment with a Human Face* concludes that in middle-income countries, where resource constraints are not so binding, "Political leadership and community participation are the requirements for success in overcoming the unavoidable opposition such policies will encounter."[4]

Political commitment is important to any kind of policy initiative. But even strong commitment must be tempered by calculations of political risk and the imperative of political survival. Protecting or promoting the interests of the poor is at best only one among many goals of leaders and governments, and it is usually a fairly low-priority concern. Vested wealthy interests are of course an obstacle to some key pro-poor measures: Land reform is the classic example. In many countries, however, elite opposition to pro-poor measures may be less crucial in shaping policies and resources than the competing claims on state resources of middle- and working-class groups—who are better off than the poor, but by no means rich, and far more organized, vocal, and active in politics.

It is a truism that poorer groups in all societies tend to be less articulate and well-connected, and to participate less through formal and informal political channels than those who are better off. But different types of political systems, different patterns of political coalitions, and variations among the poor themselves result in widely varying degrees of powerlessness or influence. The ultra-poor and the vulnerable are almost never politically active; however, local and international charitable and religious organizations lobby on their behalf and are reinforced in some countries by strong social welfare bureaucracies. External aid agencies are also playing this role with increasing vigor. Domestic and foreign advocates for the ultra-poor have often been effective in protecting and promoting relief programs, but not in prompting broad reallocations of resources and priorities. In the past few years, however, they have been attempting more far-reaching influence, as discussed in the second section of this chapter.

◦ Turning to the poor more broadly defined as the bottom third, generalizations become more hazardous. The poor so defined, acting on their own behalf, rarely exercise much influence on national policies. They are almost wholly rural, often geographically dispersed, and frequently controlled by landlords, employers, or local notables. Especially in poorer countries, however, the poor may have strong social and political ties with more politically vocal middle-decile groups, particularly where ethnic loyalties cut across class lines. Sometimes political institutions or circumstances also lend the poor, or some among them, greater political influence.

A common thread runs through many of the situations where governments give higher priority to the needs of poor people: Political salience increases where the poor are actually or potentially allied with groups in a position to threaten the government's security. If, for instance, poverty is viewed as a root cause of serious regional disaffection, governments may launch regional development programs with major anti-poverty components. Northeast Thailand is a classic example. Moreover, rural-based guerilla or terrorist movements often spur broad-gauged attacks on rural poverty, as they have in Negros Orientale in the Philippines or in Peru during the first years of Alan García's government. And a long-lived government can be influenced by memories of past threats for decades; in Indonesia, for example, government support for agriculture and for rural services and facilities in the 1970s and 1980s reflects memories of the powerful rural communist movement of the early 1960s.[5]

Similarly, governments' fear of protests often heightens the political salience of the *urban* poor. In these settings, it is rarely the poor alone who demonstrate or riot. Protests over food prices or other common triggers usually mobilize workers, students, lower-middle-class, and even middle-class groups, with some of the poor. The urban poor gain salience through their usually temporary and informal alliance with the somewhat better off.

In principle, the ability to reward politicians through the vote should be a political resource that is as or more important to the poor as the ability to threaten governments. Indeed, where turnout is large, contests are close, and economic issues are not submerged by other (frequently ethnic or religious) issues, politicians and governments tend to be more attentive to the interests of at least some poor groups: Sri Lanka, Costa Rica, Chile in the 1960s and early 1970s (and quite possibly in the 1990s), and many of India's states are among the examples. But as these cases themselves suggest and as the experience of industrialized democracies confirms, in practice, democratic governments are often even more responsive to middle and lower-middle strata than to the poor. The same principles predictably will shape the priorities of those governments turning or returning to democracy in the late 1980s and 1990s, with some variation, reflecting their center-right or center-left bases of support.

Where structural reforms are likely to directly or indirectly help some of the poor, those gains might permit a government to broaden its support base or to construct new coalitions. For example, wherever small cultivators produce much of the marketed crop, increased producer prices for agricultural goods are often noted as both a major key to increased economic efficiency and as a pro-poor benefit. But benefits to particular groups—perhaps especially poor groups—do not translate automatically into increased political support. In Ghana, for instance, cocoa farmers were the earliest and clearest gainers from the stabilization program. Since elections would reflect not only farmers' gains but also the much less improved and still very difficult conditions of the urban population, however,[6] the government has not formulated a way to capitalize on farmers' economic gains by mobilizing their political support.

Two other approaches are often urged as means to strengthen the poor: decentralization and increased use of grassroots organizations. Neither approach is unambiguously helpful. Local elites are often less progressive than national ones. Additionally, many organizations in which the poor and near-poor participate are dominated by slightly better off members, whose priorities are not necessarily the same as those of their poorer associates.

Whether the poor gain political salience as part of a larger threat to government security, as voters in highly competitive elections, or as members of community organizations, the same theme emerges: When governments respond to "popular" pressures, the poor usually benefit to the extent that their priority concerns overlap with those of the somewhat better off. If their interests diverge, the poor are not likely to gain much, and they may even lose ground.

That blunt conclusion does not rule out all possibility for accommodation. The areas of overlap may be large, depending on the degree to which the social and economic needs of middle deciles resemble those of the poor. In rural areas in poorer countries, households in the fourth, fifth, or sixth income deciles may share with poorer households a range of needs (such as more and better elementary schools and health clinics) and potential benefits (from feeder roads and better road maintenance, higher producer prices for certain crops, better varieties or improved cultivation techniques—especially for food crops). In the cities (where most households are likely to fall in the middle deciles of the national income distribution), both poor and middle deciles may spend substantial fractions of their budgets on the same food staples, rely on the same inadequate public transportation, and suffer from scarcities of medicines and trained personnel in health clinics. Certain programs clearly can benefit both categories, although their needs and capacities differ on some points (for instance, ability to pay user fees).

Depressions would seem to be the worst of times to try to introduce pro-poor measures, since the perennial competition with stronger groups intensifies as resources shrink. Yet the heightened visibility and urgency of poverty during such difficult periods often generates new support for at least temporary relief measures. Perhaps less obviously, an acute and protracted economic crisis can sometimes have effects similar to a sharp break in types of government—weakening old interests and mobilizing new ones, challenging established ways of thinking, demanding improvisation, and perhaps encouraging a sense of national solidarity in the face of adversity. In the United States and other nations during the Great Depression of the 1930s, economic crisis generated a surge of reform and innovation, including some durable pro-poor measures. Similarly, the pressures and ferment of the 1980s and quite probably the 1990s may heighten some governments' receptivity to innovation and provide more openings for reforms than more "normal" times. Policy dialogue and external support may encourage such trends.

The Politics of Pro-Poor Measures

The nub of the political problems of designing and implementing pro-poor measures is that such measures usually shift resources, directly or indirectly, away from more privileged groups. But different types of pro-poor measures have different characteristics that affect their political feasibility.

The political difficulty of pro-poor measures increases to the extent that the *resource transfer* from privileged groups is *obvious, long-term, and large* (relative to the incomes of these same privileged groups). Extending the principle that long-term transfers are more difficult than temporary ones, it is generally harder to transfer income-producing assets (land, access to higher education) than current income. The *target group* also matters; resource transfers are easier if they are targeted clearly to the deserving and appealing poor, above all children—or, alternatively, if the beneficiaries are fairly broadly targeted. Measures that require *extensive institutional changes* not only are harder administratively, but also are likely to provoke bureaucratic resistance. Finally, pro-poor measures have different implications for *political patronage and public relations*. Programs channeled mainly through private voluntary organizations (PVOs), for instance, are normally less attractive to governments than programs over which they have direct control.

These politically relevant traits vary with different categories of pro-poor measures. For this discussion, it is useful to distinguish among four categories of such measures—two short-term and two with longer time horizons:

- Compensatory programs for particularly vulnerable or hard-hit groups;
- Measures that minimize first-round losses for poor groups (rather than compensating them) during periods of austerity;
- More permanent restructuring of ongoing social services and programs to favor the poor; and
- Long-term pro-poor measures directed to productive sectors, such as selective infrastructure development, credit programs, extension services, and pricing policies.

Governments in developing nations and some of the external agencies working with those governments (most clearly the World Bank and USAID) have shifted their emphasis among these different categories in response to the economic deterioration and the ideological currents of the 1980s. The initial effect of the debt crisis was to push pro-poor programs and concerns to the "back burner." By the late 1980s, the human costs of recession and adjustment became obvious. One response has been high priority for immediate relief for the poorest and most vulnerable, and a new theme of assistance for the direct victims (not necessarily the extremely poor) of adjustment measures—mainly laid off public-sector workers. A second response has been strong pressure on the International Monetary Fund (IMF) and the World Bank from debtor governments and from pro-poor advocates to redesign stabilization and structural change programs to avoid harm to the poor. The longer-term pro-poor measures at the core of "basic needs strategies" of the 1970s are also part of the current resurgent concern about poverty in the late 1980s. In contrast to a decade ago, however, much more emphasis is now being placed on measures that will be compatible with the acute fiscal constraints expected to stretch into the 1990s. The themes of user fees, targeted subsidies, and altered priorities in social services have new prominence. Revised ideas about the roles of the state versus private markets and about the importance of international trade for growth have also shaped choices and designs of long-term pro-poor strategies—for example, focusing more attention on producer pricing policies, and putting on the defensive those who advocate food self-sufficiency strategies at the expense of export crops.

Compensatory Programs ʌ

Compensatory programs are the least politically controversial category of pro-poor action. Especially in Latin America and Asia, many long-established programs providing food aid and/or temporary employment to the needy were expanded or supplemented as recession deepened in the 1980s. Well-established social welfare programs and bureaucracies probably played a more important role in facilitating such efforts than did broader pro-poor orientations. In equity-oriented Costa Rica during the intensive stabilization drive of 1982–83, the government speedily set up a temporary (13-month) food aid program, which at its peak distributed food packets to some 40,000 families designated as needy by local committees—or roughly 1 in 12 households. In Chile, despite the absence of a broader pro-poor stance, employment programs were rapidly expanded to provide some income to roughly an eighth of the labor force in the depths of the depression of 1983, and nutrition, health, and family subsidy programs for poor children and mothers were also strengthened. Politically, the key features of compensatory programs of this kind are their targeting to the neediest, and the presumption that the entire program (or its expanded scale) is temporary and justified by acute crisis.

More ambitious, multi-faceted, short-term compensatory programs are planned or under way in a number of countries, funded mainly by external donors. The two best known are the Bolivian Emergency Social Fund (ESF) and the Ghanaian Program of Action to Mitigate the Social Consequences of Adjustment (PAMSCAD), the latter getting under way only in late 1988. The core of both programs is small local public works and social service projects to generate employment and to improve conditions. The projects are proposed and often designed and implemented by local communities or voluntary agencies. Both programs are broadly targeted to urban and rural poor and near-poor, but they also seek to serve special groups reflecting clear political concerns. ESF was intended to provide alternative employment for many of the roughly 20,000 workers who lost their jobs as the result of tin-mine closing or restructuring. (As things turned out, most of the miners had the skills to locate new jobs on their own.) PAMSCAD is earmarking about a fifth of its funds for direct compensation, counseling, and training for thousands of public sector workers trimmed from overstaffed agencies. Somewhat similar programs (usually less complex, and often combining short-term relief with longer-term development components) are planned or under discussion with the World Bank in Cameroon, Chad, Guinea-Bissau, Guinea, Madagascar, Senegal, and Sudan in Africa, and in Guatemala, Guyana, and Haiti in Latin America.[7]

The obvious and dominant political features of these programs are their largely external funding and their broad targeting. Even the modest share of domestic funding required may loom large for these particularly hard-pressed countries, but the catalytic role of local funds in bringing in far larger foreign finance is a strong political incentive. Most of these programs are also explicitly temporary, which facilitates funding by both donors and governments, although the short time frame also raises serious problems with respect to administration, quality of projects, and provision for their longer-term maintenance.[8]

Compensatory programs are not free from political controversy. A common charge is use of funds for partisan advantage. Politicians may oppose channeling funds through local communities and nongovernmental organizations (NGOs), short-circuiting their own allocation of patronage and developing alternative power centers. Government bureaucrats may also resent such channeling, since it implies doubts about their own capabilities and establishes rivals in their area of responsibility. In a few cases, such obstacles have blocked adoption of compensatory programs where World Bank staff have tried to encourage them. Usually, however, the major blocks have been financial and administrative rather than political.

A larger issue raised by compensatory programs can be assessed only in the longer run. These ambitious programs not only promise rapid results but are also politically much easier for most governments to enact than the more durable shifts in social programs and development strategy discussed later in this chapter. From the vantage point of the year 2000, will compensatory programs generated by the crisis of the 1980s be seen to have diverted governmental and external-agency resources and efforts from more enduring pro-poor measures? Or will they prove to be wedges or forerunners for more permanent efforts, by building constituencies and demonstrating techniques for reducing poverty?

Designing Adjustment Policies to Spare the Poor

Compensatory programs are often criticized as "band-aids" applied to relieve some of the damage of depression and adjustment. Their critics argue strongly for a more integral pro-poor approach to the design of adjustment measures themselves. Such an approach should be applied, they urge, at every level of adjustment choices: in the mix and phasing of macroeconomic measures and the priorities and design of sectoral policies as well as more specific programs and projects.

The call for redesigning macroeconomic packages to spare the poor has not had much impact. The overall severity of austerity measures adopted—the depth of cuts in government expenditures and subsidies, the size of tax and utility rate increases, the extent of credit tightening—broadly determines the impact on living standards. The policy-makers, however, seldom choose the severity and pace of the program, which are largely dictated by the economic situation and the availability of external finance. A more humane pace of adjustment hinges above all on less adverse resource flows. Despite all the caveats about the uses to which financing may be put, increased financing and/or a measure of debt relief remain the most powerful pro-poor instruments available; their deployment depends crucially on action by the industrial nations.

Given existing resources, different "equally severe" combinations of policies will have different distributive effects. The IMF, in particular, has been urged to assess the effects of alternative packages and to advise governments accordingly, or even to insist on their selecting more pro-poor alternatives. But distributive effects of macroeconomic measures are hard to anticipate for several reasons. In most developing countries, there are virtually no data on the "profile of poverty," including the geographic distribution, sources of income, access to services, and expenditure patterns of poor households. Even where data are a bit better, the ways in which alternative policy packages would help and hurt particular categories of poor people are complex, often ambiguous, and vary between the short and longer run. Assessment is even harder if inflation is rapid and if sharp changes in key prices (exchange rates, interest rates) are required. Particular measures—for example, increases in agricultural producer prices—may help some categories of poor people while seriously harming others.

The IMF, the World Bank, and other external agencies engaged in policy dialogue and conditionality have a special obligation to try to assess the most likely distributive effects of measures they advise or require, especially where those measures carry a direct risk for some of the poor. That obligation is now acknowledged by both institutions. The World Bank and other international agencies have launched vigorous efforts to assist governments in collecting the basic data. Efforts to improve analytic methodology are also under way.[9] But better data and methodology will both take time; meanwhile, most "damage limitation" efforts focus on components of broader packages, particularly the allocation of cuts in social expenditures and the design of subsidy reductions and wage policies.

Wage policies often reflect equity considerations—that is, they are milder for lower-paid workers—precisely because the approach carries few political risks while conveying a sense of concern for the poor. The approach relies partly on the framework of union solidarity to encourage better-paid workers to sacrifice in the interests of their poorer co-workers. As part of a broader austerity effort in Colombia in the second half of 1984, for example, average wage increases were held to 10 per cent (well below inflation), but the scale was weighted so that the highest paid workers received less than 10 per cent and the minimum wage actually increased in real terms.[10] Needless to say, the *structure* of wage cuts can favor poorer workers while the overall *level* of wage reductions shrinks workers' share of gross domestic product and cuts their consumption relatively more than that of wealthier groups.

Preferential budget cuts are often politically more difficult than wage cuts favoring poorer workers, because the resource transfer is more obvious. It is often asserted that austerity has led to particularly drastic cuts in social programs. But Hicks's study of twenty-four countries found that social programs usually were cut somewhat less than proportionately to overall expenditures,[11] although the data are not detailed enough to gauge whether those elements most important to the poor have been protected. On the revenue side of the fiscal ledger, increased charges for public services are sometimes cross-subsidized to spare poorer groups, and tax collection is often tightened to reduce evasion (mainly by the wealthy). Most rate increases, however, target those sources that are administratively simple and/or lucrative (such as excises on beer or cigarettes, and trade taxes) rather than place great emphasis on equity.

Not even aggressive design of wage and public expenditure cuts to protect low-income groups would help many of the poor. Few of the truly poor work for wages controlled or guided by the government. Many, especially in poorer countries and in rural areas, lack access to public utilities and public services. To reach them, more active pro-poor measures are needed.

c Restructuring Social Expenditures in Favor of the Poor

A longer-term and more enduring approach to protecting and promoting poorer groups in the course of adjustment is reorienting the structure of public social-sector programs. Such reorientation is a major theme in recent adjustment dialogue because it addresses *both* poverty problems and the acute fiscal crisis likely to continue in many countries into the 1990s.[12] The most frequently advocated measures include: substituting targeted for general food subsidies; restructuring education to emphasize primary facilities while containing the costs of burgeoning university programs; and expanding preventive and basic curative measures and health facilities while channeling less to hospital care. This discussion probes the *political* incentives for such reforms from the perspective of governments in power.

Shifting from General to Targeted Food Subsidies

The World Bank and the IMF have long pointed out that general subsidies benefit the non-poor far more than the poor. They advocate substituting targeted for general subsidies to protect the poor while easing fiscal drain. Despite the obvious political risks, many governments reduced or eliminated consumer subsidies in the 1980s in response to the fiscal crisis, often coupled with external pressure. But very few of them simultaneously launched or expanded targeted programs to protect the poor. This was partly due to the considerable technical and administrative difficulty of designing and setting up targeted programs. In a few instances, perhaps most clearly Zambia at the end of 1986, such problems sabotaged an attempted shift from broader to narrower subsidies. Nevertheless, political obstacles to targeted programs (separate from the risks of cutting general subsidies) are still more important deterrents than technical obstacles.

Many governments resist the introduction of improved data gathering techniques essential for tight targeting, fearing that such data will provide their opposition with new and potent ammunition. Political leaders (and sometimes the public, or parts of it) may feel that food stamps or "inferior goods" approaches to targeting demean the beneficiaries. Creating or expanding institutional machinery to implement a targeted system can also raise a host of "micro-political" and bureaucratic politics issues.

More fundamentally, governments have a strong political (as distinct from ethical) incentive to substitute targeted for general subsidies *only if the beneficiaries of targeted programs comprise a significant part of the political threat entailed in removing the general subsidy.*[13] In the two clearest cases of simultaneous substitution of targeted for general subsidies, Sri Lanka and Morocco both targeted their revised programs to broad middle strata as well as the poor.

Sri Lankan experience is particularly instructive. Sri Lanka had provided a rice subsidy (at times free rations) for the entire population since World War II. Sporadic attempts to scale back these expenditures—long a serious fiscal burden—were political disasters. In 1978–79, however, the subsidy was converted (in two steps discussed below) to a food stamp program aimed at the poorer half of the population.

Two points are salient for this discussion. First, the set of circumstances permitting the reform were most unusual. A new government—committed to a well-worked-out and broad-gauged adjustment program and skilled in political tactics—had been elected by a landslide. The opposition was decimated, and the public was ready for change after years of economic stagnation and political turmoil. External aid was heavy, the weather good, and favorable international prices brought renewed economic growth. Rice farmers, a politically important group, viewed the rice ration as a price depressant and favored its reform. Careful administrative planning facilitated implementation.

Second, despite this array of favorable factors, in democratic Sri Lanka the new targeting had to be loose. The first step, in 1978, removed the subsidy from the wealthier half of the population. The second step, in 1979, converted the ration to food stamps, and the government sought simultaneously to check the rolls and to tighten the targeting to the poorest third, while somewhat increasing the benefits. Officials knew that many households were under-reporting, especially in rural areas, where verification was difficult, but they were under strong pressure from members of parliament not to challenge declared incomes.[14] Later analyses concluded that almost 30 per cent of households in the upper half of the income distribution were receiving food stamps. Worse, an equal proportion among households in the bottom half were *not* receiving them.[15]

Inflation accelerated in the early 1980s, and by 1985 the real value of the food stamps had halved. Spurred partly by studies flagging nutritional deficiencies among the poor, the government in 1985 made a second effort to trim the food stamp rolls in order to permit increased benefits for poorer households. Again, however, strong pressure from parliament made the government back off, although special nutrition programs for the very poor were adopted.[16] Aid for the poor was acceptable; cutting the benefits of middle deciles was not.

In Morocco, consumer subsidies on various foods were removed between 1985 and 1988 as part of a broad adjustment program. By 1988, only flour, sugar, and cooking oil were still subsidized. In mid-1988, the subsidy for high-quality flour was removed, but the less refined grade remained subsidized. Related steps sought to ensure continued availability but to discourage the better off from buying the subsidized flour.[17] Adverse effects on the very poor were also cushioned by expanding established nutrition and "food for work" programs.

For this discussion, the most salient point is that, as in Sri Lanka, the targeting embraced not only the poor, but also a broad swathe of Morocco's middle strata. The grade of flour that remained subsidized had accounted for about 80 per cent of all flour milled prior to the reforms. Despite some tightening of the total quantity eligible for subsidy, it is a fair guess that the subsidized portion continues to account for much of the flour milled; freeing the price of higher-grade flour mainly affected the top two or three deciles. The broader principle is clear: If targeting is to ease political risks as well as to soften the welfare impact of subsidy reductions, the target group cannot be *only* the poor.

Restructuring Education and Other Social Sectors

From a government's perspective, restructuring social-sector expenditures may offer even fewer incentives than substituting targeted for general subsidies. Such reforms offend politically vocal groups without easing the overall fiscal bind. Most of the few successful examples entail special political circumstances or incentives. Zimbabwe restructured public spending to favor primary education and health facilities in the years after independence, between 1979–80 and 1985–86.[18] That shift reflected a sharp—indeed, revolutionary—change of regime. Moreover, while the new government was the result of a long and difficult struggle, once installed, it faced no real threat of imminent overthrow.

Indonesia provides a second example of vigorous pro-poor social-sector allocations—especially for primary schools and for village and province-level discretionary programs during the 1980s. As already mentioned, those measures were part of a broader political strategy of favoring rural groups in order to reduce risks of resurgent rural radicalism.

Major education reforms under way in Morocco and Ghana illustrate the more typical difficulties of restructuring social expenditures. Both programs emphasize expanded and improved primary education, especially in under-served rural regions. Both entail phased elimination of subsidies for university students' living expenses and books; in Ghana, this extends also to the upper secondary level. Morocco's sectoral adjustment loan with the World Bank further sought to radically slow the expansion of enrollment at the university level, from a rate varying between 6 and 10 per cent annually in the early 1980s to a ceiling of 2 per cent a year.[19]

The directly "pro-poor" aspects of these programs drew both support and criticism.[20] However, intense resistance predictably focused on efforts to withdraw benefits from university students and to limit expansion of enrollment in Morocco. In 1987, after the first of two rounds of baccalaureate examinations produced an unusually low pass ratio in Morocco, political intervention from the highest levels led to a much looser second round and an increase in enrollment of over 25 per cent. In Ghana, reduced subsidies for university students provoked strident student protests in both 1987 and 1988, causing the campuses to be closed.

Neither Ghana nor Morocco has abandoned the reforms, and both governments may nibble away subsidies at higher levels, perhaps in tandem with gradual upgrading of quality. Restructuring of social programs, even more than shrinking food subsidies, will be an ongoing struggle over resource allocations, with the non-poor usually holding most of the political cards.

Where extensive external finance is available, social-sector programs can be restructured as part of a general rehabilitation of social services. Discussions between the Government of Jamaica and the World Bank begun in 1988 regarding a Social Adjustment Program fit this description. Elements of the proposed program focus on the urban and rural poor, but much of it serves a very broad constituency—obviously making it very attractive politically. But financing for such efforts is not likely beyond a fortunate few countries, particularly small ones.

The global campaign to improve children's health with simple, low-cost techniques, spearheaded by UNICEF, demonstrates a much more widely applicable approach to the partial reorientation of social expenditures. Since 1985, UNICEF has gained the cooperation of a great many governments for vigorous campaigns of innoculation, accompanied by the dissemination of information and simple materials for oral rehydration, growth monitoring, and encouragement of breast-feeding, resulting in dramatically improved children's health.[21] Similar large-scale programs of growth monitoring and targeted nutrition were under way earlier in the state of Tamilnadu in India, as well as in the poorer rural areas of Colombia from the mid-1970s to 1982.

From the perspective of cooperating governments, such programs have several attractive political features. They are inexpensive compared to many other social sector expenditures, and the unit cost per beneficiary is extremely low. External agencies have covered a large share of the costs, including the vaccines. The campaigns focus on children—always an appealing target. The goal is usually to reach 80 per cent of the child population, which means that the campaigns are *not* tightly targeted to the poorest strata but also benefit children in middle-decile income groups. Governments can expect political benefits from the extensive publicity associated with the drives in each country. The approach has produced impressive results. But the same "special campaign" excitement that contributes to effectiveness also raises questions about sustainability—particularly since local resources for the efforts in specific countries often have been co-opted from other parts of the health care system, the military, or whatever agencies could provide vehicles and loudspeakers. The "special campaign" approach is probably not a viable model for many other goals, to the extent that these are more costly and/or are not largely externally financed, demand more complex institutional changes, target less appealing groups, or target more narrowly.

Long-Term Pro-Poor Measures Directed to Productive Sectors

Reorienting social services to better serve the poor and near-poor is only one set of approaches to the broader long-term goal of pro-poor development. The approach is singled out in this discussion because of its close links to fiscal austerity and its special prominence in the context of adjustment programs. This short chapter cannot attempt to summarize the extensive writing on other aspects of long-term pro-poor strategies,[22] beyond noting that the political considerations already discussed apply equally to these longer-run measures. For example, land reforms are usually extremely difficult because they entail transparent, permanent, and large transfers from rich to poor; they also require considerable supporting institutional change. In contrast, credit programs directed to the poor—another way to increase access to productive assets—are less difficult politically because the transfers are less obvious, more diffused, and smaller relative to the wealth and income of those footing the bill. Nor do credit programs involve the permanent loss of assets by better off groups. The fiercest opponents are often money lenders or others already providing credit on much less favorable terms.

More broadly, political difficulties tend to increase to the degree that pro-poor measures offer not merely temporary relief but more durable benefits. This reality does not rule out hope for change, but it does caution against inflated expectations of rapid progress if governments and international financial institutions increased their attention to the poor. While efficiency and social justice argue for targeting benefits to the poor, political incentives point toward broader targeting that reaches some of the more politically influential middle deciles. Tight targeting of more than compensatory benefits may be a realistic option only for governments that do not need popular support.

Pro-Poor Measures, Perceived Equity, and Political Sustainability

Lightening adjustment burdens for the poor is a goal in itself, but it is also often urged as a means of increasing the political sustainability of adjustment efforts. Is that assumed linkage valid?

Clearly much of the resistance to adjustment measures is unrelated to burdens on the poor. Industrialists concerned about tariff cuts, businessmen pinched by restrictive monetary policy, commercial farmers reacting to reduced subsidies for fertilizers or credit, employees of parastatals being reorganized or privatized—all of these groups bitterly oppose aspects of adjustment and will not be mollified by pro-poor measures.

Popular protest is also a growing threat to adjustment efforts, through urban riots such as those in March 1989 in Venezuela as well as through elections. "Populist" candidates have recently won major local elections in Brazil and national elections in Jamaica; shaken the foundations of the Institutional Revolutionary Party (PRI) in Mexico; and appear likely to win national contests in 1989 in Argentina and Brazil. In Nigeria, the lengthy series of elections between 1989 and 1991 as the country moves toward full democracy are likely to raise similar challenges to adjustment measures.

These pressures come as much, or more, from middle deciles and from (wealthier) "middle" classes as from the poor. Indeed, the intensity of the political challenge reflects its broad social base. The poor are least able to sustain any losses, but in many countries in the 1980s, the middle deciles, particularly in cities, have suffered the largest losses in income and living standards. They are less needy, but are more aggrieved. To take but one example, in Mexico, formal-sector workers (as in most other countries, not among the poorest) saw their average real wages erode by roughly half between 1982 and 1988.

For the middle deciles, "equitable" adjustment means relief for them as well as for the very poor; the *equity* issue is not the same as the *poverty* issue. Indeed, many in the middle deciles may be less concerned about the suffering of the poor—after all, the poor are a long-standing feature of the social landscape—than they are incensed about the failure of the wealthy to carry their share of the burdens of the 1980s. The international dimensions of the equity issue also loom ever larger; middle deciles see medical facilities and schools for their children deteriorating while their governments pay staggering sums to foreign bankers.

To put the point more harshly: In most countries, the political difficulties of economic adjustment would be much reduced if employment, real incomes, and public services were improved for the middle deciles *regardless of what happened to the bottom third.* The call for "adjustment with a human face" is interpreted more broadly in most developing nations than in the rich nations and the development institutions. It is a call for adjustment that stresses growth more and austerity less, a respite not only or primarily for the poor but for the "popular classes." That call requires shifts in net resource flows between North and South, not solely within Southern nations.

Some Implications for Action

1. *Sharply targeted pro-poor measures should be pursued mainly to relieve suffering and promote social justice.* Their contribution to political sustainability is likely to be modest.

2. *Sizable compensatory programs should be designed, so far as possible, to serve as wedges or models for more durable pro-poor efforts rather than as substitutes for or diversions from such efforts.* This criterion may bear on financing, choice of implementing agencies, the extent and nature of public participation in choosing and implementing projects, and other design elements.

3. *It is important to be aware of the implications of arbitrary definitions of "poverty" for welfare and politics.* Analysis and data collection by external agencies, or such efforts by governments with support from external agencies, should not focus narrowly on the bottom third. From both welfare and political perspectives, it is important to keep track of trends and conditions among the middle deciles as well.

4. *While temporary compensation programs may be fairly tightly targeted, longer-term pro-poor measures may need to also extend some benefits to the less poor to be politically acceptable and sustainable.* Data beginning to be generated by the World Bank's Living Standards Measurement Surveys and other survey-based efforts may permit a deliberate search for overlapping interests between some of the bottom third and the slightly better off strata. As a practical matter, neither food subsidies targeted by commodity or neighborhood, nor most public facilities (schools, clinics, water standpipes) can be directed exclusively to the poor. This is probably an advantage rather than a drawback.

5. *Withdrawing benefits from middle-class groups usually should be gradual, accompanied by painstaking explanation and dialogue, and timed with attention to economic trends and political events that might*

cushion the impact or divert attention. The timing of such measures should also be considered in the context of other adjustment measures that may generate resistance from the same groups. John Waterbury (in Chapter 1) stresses the same principle: Avoid actions that antagonize several major groups within the population at the same time.

6. *Pro-poor measures, like most other aspects of structural adjustment (as distinct from short-run austerity measures) depend for effective implementation on broad understanding and commitment within the government itself.* Continuing dialogue with external agencies, including improved data, analysis, and information about other countries' experiences with similar efforts, may build a basis for future action even when there is little immediate response. The new willingness, often eagerness, of many governments to set up systems to gather living-standard data regularly may be a crucial breakthrough for long-term pro-poor development efforts. Once available, numbers are politically difficult to ignore.

Notes

[1] More precisely, the "ultra poor" are defined as those who spend roughly 70 to 80 per cent of their incomes on food (the remainder an irreducible minimum spent on other needs) but who cannot buy average caloric requirements for their age, size, and level of activity, so that they are undernourished (and usually malnourished). Michael Lipton, *The Poor and the Poorest: Some Interim Findings,* World Bank Discussion Paper No. 25 (Washington, D.C., 1988).
[2] The World Bank has also developed much more refined measures of poverty. In the late 1970s, considerable effort was devoted to developing an appropriate "poverty line" (varying, of course, in different countries) for each of many countries. Currently the Bank is working with a number of governments to set up periodic Living Standards Measurement Surveys (LSMS) to identify and provide information on the poor. But recent analyses of the state of the poor in each of the Bank's major regional departments used the poorest 30 per cent as a starting point for discussion, and the analyses based on data from the earliest LSMS returns (from the Ivory Coast and Peru) gave special attention to the poorest 10 per cent and 30 per cent.
[3] Our language often trips us up: The so-called "middle classes" in most developing countries are not part of the middle deciles, but fall in the top 20 per cent or even 10 per cent.
[4] Giovanni Andrea Cornia, Richard Jolly, and Frances Stewart, eds., *Adjustment with a Human Face: Protecting the Vulnerable and Promoting Growth* (Oxford, England: Clarendon Press, 1987), p. 297.
[5] Wing Thye Woo, "Adding Economic Methodology to the Analysis of State-Society Relations: An Application to Indonesia." Unpublished manuscript (University of California at Davis, January 1989).
[6] See Thomas M. Callaghy, "Between State and Market: The Politics of Adjustment in Ghana, Zambia, and Nigeria," in Joan Nelson, ed., *Economic Crisis and Policy Choice: The Politics of Adjustment in the Third World* (Princeton, N.J.: Princeton University Press, forthcoming, 1990); and Emmanuel Gyimah-Boadi, "Economic Recovery and Politics in the PNDC's Ghana." Paper prepared for a conference on the politics of structural adjustment programs, 31 March–1 April 1989, Institute of Development Studies, Sussex University, Sussex, England.
[7] Elaine Zuckerman, "Compensatory Programs: Redressing the Social Costs of Adjustment," Draft paper (Washington, D.C: The World Bank, February 1989).

[8] Zuckerman, ibid.; also Soniya Carvalho, Robert Liebenthal, Peter Nicholas, Helena Ribe, and Elaine Zuckerman, "How Adjustment Programs Can Help the Poor: The Experience of the World Bank," World Bank Paper (Washington, D.C.: The World Bank, November 1988), pp. 14–16.

[9] See, for example, Ravi Kanbur, "The Implications of Adjustment Programs for Poverty: Conceptual Issues and Analytical Framework." Paper prepared for an internal International Monetary Fund seminar on the implications of adjustment programs for poverty groups, 29 November–2 December 1988.

[10] Barbara Stallings, "Politics and Economic Crisis: A Comparative Study of Chile, Peru, and Colombia," in Nelson, ed., *Economic Crisis and Policy Choice*, op. cit.

[11] Norman L. Hicks, "Expenditure Reductions in Developing Countries Revisited," Unpublished manuscript (Washington, D.C.: The World Bank, February 1989). See also Hicks, "Expenditure Reductions in High-Debt Countries," *Finance & Development*, Vol. 26, No. 1 (March 1989), pp. 35–37, which focuses on a smaller sample.

[12] The introduction in the 1980s of policy-based lending, including sector loans, also provides the World Bank (and to some extent other external agencies) with a new instrument for encouraging and supporting revised social-sector priorities.

[13] The poor or near-poor may not be part of the political threat for two quite different reasons. The more obvious reason is disempowerment: a political system in which they have very little weight. Even where the *urban* near-poor have some impact, they may not pose a risk because they are not benefiting from the general subsidy. This often happens because the government cannot afford to purchase enough of the subsidized staple to meet more than a fraction of the demand. That fraction rarely reaches the poor or near-poor.

[14] M. D. D. Pieris, "Decade of Food Policy Reforms: Sri Lanka, 1977–87." Paper prepared for the Seminar on Economic Policy Change and Governmental Process, sponsored by the Korean Development Institute and the Economic Development Institute of the World Bank, 9–12 November 1987, Seoul, Korea, p. 33.

[15] Neville Edirisinghe, "Food Subsidy Changes in Sri Lanka: The Short-Run Effect on the Poor," in Per Pinstrup-Anderson, ed., *Food Subsidies in Developing Countries* (Baltimore, Md.: Johns Hopkins University Press, 1988), p. 260.

[16] Pieris, "Decade of Food Policy Reforms," op. cit., p. 53.

[17] Mills were authorized to increase the extraction rate, producing a slightly darker, more nutritious but less appealing flour. The total amount of subsidized flour authorized for production was reduced by 40 per cent (though it is not clear that the previous and larger quota had been fully produced); in principle, mills in poorer districts received larger quotas. To reduce fiscal pressure, the price of subsidized flour was increased by roughly 10–12 per cent. Also linked to these changes were arrangements to clear government arrears owed to millers.

[18] Cornia, Jolly, and Stewart, *Adjustment with a Human Face*, op. cit., p. 176.

[19] Both the Moroccan and Ghanaian education reforms are complex, multifaceted programs that seek to reorient curricula and improve quality and cost-effectiveness in many ways. This short discussion focuses only on the politics of the pro-poor shift in resources.

[20] Among the Moroccan elite, there was muted criticism that increased basic literacy risked increasing the alienation of semi-educated youth in the absence of expanded employment opportunities. In Ghana, middle- and upper-middle-class parents were upset at the introduction of mandatory basic technical education in primary schools.

[21] A range of possible new goals are listed in UNICEF's report on *The State of the World's Children, 1989* (Oxford, England: Oxford University Press for UNICEF, 1989).

[22] See, for example, John P. Lewis and contributors, *Strengthening the Poor: What Have We Learned?* (New Brunswick, N.J.: Transaction Books in cooperation with the Overseas Development Council, 1988). On the politics of longer-term pro-poor measures, see William Ascher, *Scheming for the Poor: The Politics of Redistribution in Latin America* (Cambridge, Mass.: Harvard University Press, 1984); and Albert O. Hirschman, *Journeys Toward Progress* (New York: Twentieth Century Fund, 1963).

Chapter 5

Toward State Capability and Embedded Liberalism in the Third World: Lessons for Adjustment

Thomas M. Callaghy

> We were faced with two options, which we debated very fiercely before we finally chose this path. I know because I participated very actively in these debates. Two choices: We had to maneuver our way around the naiveties of leftism, which has a sort of disdain for any talk of financial discipline, which seeks refuge in some vague concept of structuralism in which everything doable is possible. . . . Moreover, [we had to find a way between] this naivete and the crudities and rigidities and dogma of monetarism, which behaves as if once you set the monetary incentives everybody will do the right thing and the market will be perfect.[1]
>
> —Kwesi Botchwey
> *Minister for Finance and Economic*
> *Planning, Government of Ghana*

Successful economic adjustment requires linking *economic logic*—the measures needed to pursue economic efficiency in both the international and domestic arenas—and *political logic*—the measures needed to assure domestic stability—in ways that allow them to positively reinforce each other. Under the right conditions, the state can play a central role in this task. As Minister Botchwey's words indicate, leaders of developing countries are becoming intensely aware of the difficulty of positively linking these dynamics and the often precarious balancing act this process requires of the state. This chapter first discusses the historical linkage between economic and political logic in economic change and the way they are currently linked for developed industrial

countries in the contemporary international political economy as captured by the notion of "embedded liberalism." The chapter concentrates,
however, on the problems that Third World states undergoing economic
adjustment encounter in effectively mediating between economic and
political logic, and on the domestic and international obstacles to
extending embedded liberalism to the Third World. The focus will be on
two types of state-economy interactions, requiring two types of state
capabilities: the bureaucratic and the political. Both are necessary for
effective and sustained economic adjustment, which requires a delicate
and tension-filled balance between state and market.

Economic Adjustment and a Balanced Tension Between State and Market

Attempting to cope with the Third World debt crisis, Western states and
actors have tried to apply the "monoeconomics" of the dominant neo-
orthodox view of development to countries dependent on the International Monetary Fund (IMF) and the World Bank. The two central tenets of this view are export-led growth and a minimalist state, and its
major instrument of reform is the market. The new orthodoxy perceives
the state itself as a key obstacle to development, whereas the structural-
ists have found impediments in the internal and external socioeconomic
structure and the political relations produced by it.

Yet an orthodox paradox exists: External actors are attempting to
use what they consider the key obstacle to development—the state—as
the primary weapon in their struggle to reform Third World political
economies. How can governments be convinced to change policies and
institutions that neo-orthodoxy believes to be economically damaging
or irrational, but which these governments consider politically rational
and deeply rooted in local political economy and history? Except for trying to remove the state from the economy, neo-orthodoxy does not offer a
theory of state reform. This has proved a major impediment to effective
economic adjustment in the Third World.[2]

The orthodox paradox is also ironic, in that the Fund and the Bank
do not always practice what they preach. Much of their activity actually
reinforces the role of the state through attempts to improve monitoring,
data-gathering, and analytic and planning capabilities; the provision of
technical assistance and training missions; parastatal reform; and even
the privatization of state-owned enterprises, which, if it is to be done
effectively, requires a capable state apparatus. The very fact that the
Fund, the Bank, and Western countries funnel resources through the
state leads to a concern with policy formulation, implementation,
assessment, and other governmental functions. In practice, then, exter-

nal agencies have begun to recognize the central role of the state and the need to balance state and market forces and economic and political logics. But rhetoric and policy design often fail to reflect these insights.

Historically the state has always played an integral role in successful economic development, as the pioneering work of Weber, Polanyi, and Gerschenkron demonstrated. More recent studies by Douglass North, Albert Hirschman, and others have further punctured the myth that the original rise of capitalism in Europe was purely or even predominantly a *private* matter of the market and of the development of technology.[3] In reality it took a properly balanced tension between emerging bureaucratic states and consolidating markets to foster the conditions neccessary for capitalism to flourish. As one recent assessment has stressed:

> An effective bureaucratic machinery is the key to the state's capacity to intervene. In order for the capitalist state to engage in economic transformation, however, the workings of this machinery must link up with the workings of the market. . . . The more that social relations . . . approach contractual market exchange and bureaucratic organization, the greater is the likelihood of effective state intervention, since market exchange and bureaucratic organization are major institutional forms that encourage instrumental behavior and protect it by institutional differentiation and insulation. . . . The increasing penetration of civil society by market exchange and bureaucratic organization provides a partial explanation for the greatly increased, if not unlimited, transformative capacity the modern state displays in contrast to patrimonial rule in agrarian societies.[4]

Yet the development of state bureaucratic capacity involves a "delicate, long-term process of institution building, which makes it much less probable that a given state will have the bureaucracy it needs when it needs it. . . . Such institutional constructions are likely to require decades, if not generations, to become established."[5] In short, as Kenneth Waltz has noted, necessities do not make possibilities.[6] In much of the current policy work on the development of state capacity in Third World countries, however, there is a strong voluntarist or architectonic streak that argues that state capacity can be "built" as part of a policy imperative. The historical record belies this assumption.

The impressive economic development of East Asian countries such as Korea and Taiwan has been used by some to illustrate the myth of the marginal role of the state. More careful study of these cases demonstrates that economic liberalization and export-oriented development demand a semi-strong and capable state. Recent research on the Latin American newly industrializing countries (NICs) points in the same direction.[7] In some of the East Asian and Latin American cases, proper market incentives (especially foreign exchange, interest, and credit policies), trade liberalization, and conservative fiscal and monetary policies have played a significant role. However, these successful exporters have also maintained high levels of protection against imports of competing goods, parastatal sectors which included import-substitution activities, and a very interventionist role for the state. In these cases, the key indeed has been maintaining a balanced tension between state and market.

Speaking of Korea, Haggard and Kaufman point out that, in addition to adopting appropriate liberalization policies, the government also

> developed a sophisticated *organization* for providing market information, assisting firms with foreign buyers and monitoring export behavior, in some cases down to the level of the individual firm. In addition, the transition to export-led growth was preceded by fundamental institutional changes in the structure of economic decision-making.[8]

This also entailed eliminating corruption and other forms of rent-seeking behavior, eliminating old political networks, and creating highly centralized and autonomous decisionmaking structures in which technocrats played the crucial role and with which domestic business groups and international actors communicated regularly and in detail.

The main task, in short, is not "getting the state out"—as much of the IMF, World Bank, and Western country rhetoric implies—but finding the state's appropriate role for fostering economic growth and development via both state and private sectors.

A Balanced Tension Between Economics and Politics: Embedded Liberalism

The need for a balanced tension between a bureaucratic state and the market is key not only for the economic logic of change, but also for its political logic. Most Northern states have pursued this balance in practice, if not in rhetoric, for quite some time. The dominant political economy among Western industrial countries in the postwar period points to the importance of the *political* link between state and market. It is a central point of this chapter that this *political* link is as important for the effectiveness of economic adjustment in Third World states as it has been for the prosperity, stability, and adjustment of Northern states over the last forty years.

Free-market principles have not in fact dominated the political economies of the industrial West since World War II. Instead, the prevailing political economy has been a form of compromise called "embedded liberalism," which involves the use of state power simultaneously in the interests of both domestic social stability and well-being and international economic adjustment.[9] At the international level, market forces have been permitted to move toward comparative advantage and adjustment. Within industrial countries, state power has been employed to varying degrees to restructure the economy and minimize and buffer the disruptive domestic social consequences of free markets at the international level as trade, finance, production, and technology have evolved. As a result, relatively open international economic policies and domestic political stability and prosperity achieved through state intervention coexist in a strained and uneasy balance, mediated by state politics.

The compromise of the postwar political economy is sometimes viewed as liberalism with lots of cheating. But the "cheating" is in fact an inherent and defining characteristic of the system. In other words, the international economic liberalism is real, but it is "compromised" by being "embedded" in the political and economic realities of domestic state-society relations. International economic efficiency is not sacrificed to domestic political stability, nor vice versa; a modus vivendi is established through embedded liberalism.

The compromise of embeddded liberalism has not, however, been extended to the Third World.[10] Developed countries have pressed Third World countries to adopt open economies without embedding these policies in the realities of domestic state-society relations. As a result, the number of successful cases of economic adjustment is quite small. As the exigencies of economic reform have become increasingly clear over time, however, the Northern actors most involved in the process—the Fund, the Bank, and some Western aid agencies—have begun to realize that liberalization without attention to domestic political stability is likely to prevent successful economic adjustment, thereby threatening crucial systemic and individual Western country interests. A number of Third World leaders are also beginning to see the wisdom of some form of embedded liberal compromise, for without some liberalization, their economies cannot gain any room for maneuver in the current international political economy. Many Western governments and legislatures, however, have been slower to perceive and act upon this reality. They have underestimated the need for the development of Third World bureaucratic and technical capabilities necessary to carry out reforms and have usually assumed that political capabilities boil down to a matter of mustering sufficient will on the part of political leaders.

Economic Adjustment and Variations in State Capability

The ability of Third World governments to engage in sustained economic adjustment—caught as they are between strong and often contradictory internal and external pressures and economic and political logics—depends in large part on the technocratic and bureaucratic capabilities of the state apparatus and the ability of leaders to use these capabilities effectively. This means coping with complex two-level negotiating "games"—economic and political games played simultaneously at domestic and international levels.[11] The success or failure of adjustment efforts to a large degree depends on a government's ability to insulate itself from—and buffer against and adjust to—threatening political, societal, and international pressures that might prevent the inherent economic logic of the adjustment process from coming into play to the extent necessary. This requires the policy leeway, resources, statecraft skill, technocratic and bureaucratic capabilities, and coercion necessary to make *and* break strategic compromises with key actors based on careful monitoring of the adjustment process in all of its stages.

One prerequisite for reform, for example, the perception of an economic crisis, is directly affected by the level and sophistication of data-gathering, analytical, and technocratic capabilities. Early and accurate warning of difficulties is very important. Leaders can choose to ignore technocratic advice, but its existence and political weight can greatly facilitate adjustment; its absence markedly increases dependence on external actors and makes it much more difficult to act simultaneously—and effectively—on both the economic and the political fronts and at both the international and domestic levels.

Much the same argument holds for the ability of a government to formulate and bargain with external and internal actors about adjustment policies and then to implement these. Leaders need to rely on, insulate, and protect the technocratic staff while keeping it informed of the political effects of its adjustment policies on both domestic and external actors. The effective operation of a technocratic core is largely determined by its size; its level of technical and administrative capability; the quality and availability of data; as well as the technocratic staff's own depth, cohesiveness, continuity over time, and the degree to which it is allowed to interact and bargain with both external and internal actors. The technocratic staff's insulation, political awareness, influence, and level of interaction with external and internal actors can vary over time given the statecraft skills of the leadership and the political impact of attempted reforms on the groups most affected by them.

The nature and use of an adjusting country's technocratic and bureaucratic capabilities are directly affected by the behavior of external actors and the resources they provide. The greater the number of external actors and Third World officials who engage in effective dialogue and learn to pay attention to the load, timing, pace, and sequencing of conditionality and the fine-tuning of policies, the greater the chances of sustained implementation (on this issue, see Miles Kahler, Chapter 6 in this volume).

In addition, sufficient and timely resource flows are required. These can come from diverse sources—export earnings, the IMF and the World Bank, bilateral assistance, debt rescheduling or reduction, new lending, and indigenous and external investment—but they *must* come. The ability to use these resources effectively is, however, seriously open to question in many countries; this has been a major factor affecting the flow of bilateral assistance, direct foreign investment, and international bank lending to much of Africa. The collapse of Zambia's economic adjustment program in 1987 was, for example, in large part attributable to insufficient resource flows from outside—due to external actors' doubts that Zambia had the capacity to sustain reforms.

Technocratic and bureaucratic capabilities vary considerably from country to country—as well as from region to region—reflecting different levels of overall development, political structures, and historical legacies. For our purposes, a recent World Bank statement about the role of the government in the design of adjustment programs applies equally to variations in overall technocratic and bureaucratic capacity: "The government's role has tended to be the greatest in Asia and Latin America, somewhat less in EMENA (Middle Eastern and North African) countries, and weakest in Sub-Saharan Africa."[12] Two broad groups of cases will be discussed here: (1) countries possessing significant levels of technocratic and bureaucratic capability, particularly the newly industrializing countries of East Asia and Latin America, and (2) countries with markedly limited abilities, especially those of Sub-Saharan Africa.

For countries with considerable capabilities, the primary issue is the ability to use them effectively in the two-level negotiating games of economic adjustment. At the international level, this entails bargaining with external actors for policy flexibility and resources sufficient to allow the development of some form of embedded liberalism. At the domestic level, the major dilemma has been one of insulating the technocratic staff and policies required for adjustment while buffering the socio-political impact of implementing such policies. In short, it is a search for effective ways to link economic and political logics.

If significant levels of technocratic and bureaucratic capability do not exist, as in much of Sub-Saharan Africa, the two-level bargaining becomes much more complex and difficult, requiring different actor roles, more resources, a slower pace, and more cautious policy sequencing. Limited capacity, for example, must be compensated for through the use of expatriate personnel, which is both politically sensitive and often of limited utility. In short, these countries face the dilemma of simultaneously creating the required capabilities while defending them from pervasive and powerful countervailing political pressures.

State Capability, Insulation, and Politics

The Cases of Chile and Mexico

Chile and Mexico are two cases in which regimes with relatively high levels of technocratic and bureaucratic capability and substantial insulation—but quite different political structures—attempted to implement orthodox economic adjustment programs, with interesting results for the notion of embedded liberalism. The major lesson is that, despite their capabilities and insulation, they had to engage in important political and economic buffering or pay a high price for not doing so.

Despite its high degree of insulation (based on a very repressive military control structure) and significant technocratic and bureaucratic capabilities, the Pinochet government in Chile nonetheless had to deviate from its strict orthodox liberalism of the 1970s to buffer sociopolitical tensions created by market forces that threatened sustained economic adjustment.[13] Beginning in 1982, growing political pressure increasingly constrained technocratic economic logic. In the context of an economic slowdown, the effects of unrestricted market forces—including insolvent businesses, failed banks, and collapsing farms—threatened the unity and very survival of the regime. Confronting the political limits of "automatic adjustment" in 1983 and 1984, the government reluctantly increased state intervention to protect key elements of the ruling coalition, to maintain the unity of the military regime, and to dampen persistent political protests. Measures included selective reflation, increased protectionism (including higher tariffs), huge subsidies to banks and large corporations, loan bail-outs, and special treatment for the construction and agricultural sectors.

The economy responded, and the political protests temporarily died down. In 1985, a new minister of finance, Hernán Büchi, sought a balanced tension between the earlier laissez-faire model and the recent state interventions. According to Barbara Stallings, "the almost universal shorthand is that Büchi is a more 'pragmatic' and 'flexible' version of the Chicago Boys."[14] His synthesis was "a long-term model resting on a small state and open economy, but a short-term model that is more interventionist."[15] This activist economic approach combined with a more open personal style allowed Büchi to successsfully conduct the two-level negotiations with key coalition partners: external actors who provided some resources and policy leeway and domestic business groups that provided badly needed support. Contending factions of the military were reunited in the process.

Out of political necessity, the Pinochet government moved in the direction of an authoritarian form of *limited* embedded liberalism. While this was a relatively successful economic strategy that brought the state back in, it was made posssible by the tight control of the military regime and the high level of technocratic and bureaucratic state capability. Sustained adjustment under a more open and participatory regime may well require a significantly broader form of embedded liberalism.

In Mexico, under the "PRI" (Institutional Revolutionary Party), a stable, de facto single-party regime has existed in Mexico for decades and has long maintained a delicate balancing act between contending social forces and political and economic logics.[16] By Third World standards, Mexico has had quite high levels of technocratic and bureaucratic state capability and insulation. Since the 1950s, the Mexican state has developed and sustained an impressive core of financially orthodox technocrats, located primarily in the Central Bank and the Treasury Department. This system provided growth and stability in Mexico from the mid-1950s through the 1960s.

In the early 1970s, however, strains over distributive issues began to appear in reaction to a move away from the PRI's populist and reformist roots of the previous fifteen years. As a result, Mexico moved once again in a more reformist direction—especially with regard to land, labor, and social policy—first under Luis Echeverría from 1970 to 1976, and then under José López Portillo from 1976 to 1982, all well within the structure of PRI dominance. This reformist and expansionary tendency produced fiscal pressures due to the growth of the state enterprise sector and increased social expenditures. These pressures were temporarily relieved by the oil boom and by external borrowing.

In the 1970s, Central Bank and Treasury officials and other technocrats, while still retaining importance in the state apparatus and the PRI leadership, lost the dominance they had enjoyed in the earlier period—especially as new bureaucratic power centers developed in the expanded state enterprise sector and in the new "super-ministry" of planning and investment. These new bureaucratic strongholds reinforced the expansionary trends.

At the same time, powerful new private business interests, particularly those based in the north of the country, became concerned about the renewed populist direction of the 1970s; state-business tensions became quite strong in the early 1980s. By the end of 1982, Mexico was in a major economic crisis, touching off the Third World "debt bomb" in the process, and it had a new IMF agreement. It also had a new president, Miguel de la Madrid. The crisis—and the very powerful external pressures that it produced—led the new Mexican government to intensify its already orthodox liberal leanings.

Under de la Madrid, a technocratic "countercoup" took place, albeit well within the PRI control structure. A technocrat himself, de la Madrid appointed fellow technocrats to all key policy positions and consistently stuck to a neo-orthodox liberal line while attempting to juggle a very delicate negotiation with domestic and external actors. This strategy was reinforced by the insulation built into the PRI system, the tradition of strong executive authority, the increased power of northern Mexican business interests, and strong external pressure accompanied by important resource support and some policy leeway.

But as the July 1988 presidential elections and the resulting political crisis demonstrated, even with these strong facilitating factors, the political costs of pursuing orthodox economic solutions were very high indeed. The PRI was very badly shaken. As in Chile, orthodox liberal trends had gone too far to be politically sustainable, and had threatened the very existence of the PRI system. Polarization remains a real possibility, especially as the economic payoff of liberalization has not been as strong as in Chile. If liberal economic adjustment is to be sustained, movement toward a more systematic form of embedded liberalism may well be needed. Whether the Brady Plan, Japan's new willingness to play a major role, and Mexico's new IMF and World Bank programs (announced in April 1989) will facilitate a move in this direction remains to be seen.

The Cases of Brazil and Argentina

Two other Latin American states with high levels of technocratic and bureaucratic capability sought to link economic and political logics through non-orthodox adjustment strategies. Drawing on already well developed technocratic skills outside the state sector that had devised new policy responses to inflation, Brazil and Argentina in the mid-1980s announced heterodox shock programs designed to contain raging inflation. Such coherent alternative strategies have not been produced in the African context because sufficient data-gathering, analytic, and technocratic capabilities do not exist in either the state or private sectors.

In Brazil and Argentina, heterodox proposals were very attractive to new political leaders because they appeared to avoid key political dilemmas raised by orthodox adjustment. The Brazilian attempt collapsed: The orthodox fiscal and monetary brakes required to make such a strategy work over time were never implemented because of their political cost. The heterodox strategy was sabotaged by the very political logic that made it so attractive in the first place. Ironically, the Argentine program worked better initially because Argentina was more dependent on the IMF, which insisted that more orthodox brakes be built into the program from the outset.

These four Latin American cases demonstrate that, even with relatively high levels of technocratic and bureaucratic capability, it is difficult to maintain the balanced tension between the state and the market. This is true whether a government pushes too far in the direction of neo-orthodoxy or too far away from it.

Compensating for Weak State Capabilities: Dependence, Politics, and Efficacy

The combination of a desperate need for resources and weak technocratic and bureaucratic state capabilities has led some Third World countries, especially those in Sub-Saharan Africa, to depend heavily on external actors for "advice" and the policy conditionality and monitoring that go with it. Attempts to compensate for weak state capabilities take place in all phases of the economic adjustment process: crisis perception, data-collection and analysis, and the formulation and implementation of adjustment policies. The compensation process usually produces considerable political tension and greatly increases the complexity and difficulty of playing the two-level "games" of economic adjustment and moving toward some form of embedded liberalism.

The Case of Zambia

External actors generally, but the IMF and the World Bank in particular, have long attempted to convince reluctant Third World governments of the need for economic adjustment. In Zambia, for example, external agencies tried throughout the 1970s to convince government officials that they needed to make significant structural changes to adjust to reduced copper earnings and to alter politically driven but economically inefficient policies. As in many other countries, this advice was not heeded until the full impact of the economic crisis of the late 1970s and early 1980s was felt. Even basic measures such as the creation of counter-cyclical reserve mechanisms for copper and the maintenance of infrastructure and productive capacity were not taken. There was even less understanding of the changes under way in the world economy. Political logic clearly controlled decisionmaking despite the valiant efforts of a few isolated technocrats to make their voices heard. During this period, however, the World Bank and other external agencies began to collect data and conduct background studies, which became very important when they later took the lead in formulating adjustment policies for Zambia and countries like it.[17]

For most of Africa, the IMF and the World Bank have played the dominant role in the formulation of stabilization and structural adjustment programs in the 1980s. Because of the African countries' high levels of dependence on foreign finance and expertise, external participation was great and led to the formal adoption of quite broad reform programs. The degree to which policy "advice" is effective depends on several key variables: a country's technical and bargaining capabilities; the size, unity, and continuity of a country's economic team; the support, insulation, and political advice provided to this team by the ruling group; the degree of centralized executive authority; the extent to which the program is perceived to be externally imposed; and the level of coalitional support for the adjustment effort.

In Zambia, the IMF and the World Bank worked with several talented individuals, but the capabilities of the rest of the economic staff were very thin. As a result, the Fund and the Bank conducted the necessary studies and analysis, established the basic framework and designed policies to fit it, and guided the negotiations. Without these external efforts, a coherent neo-orthodox adjustment program could not have been put together. But many Zambians felt that the Fund and the Bank had become the de facto finance ministry in Zambia. The Zambian economic team was often not unified, its members were rotated frequently, and it received little understanding or support from political elites. Indeed, the reforms threatened key elements of the ruling coalition, especially civil servants and the parastatals, and aroused considerable popular protest. It is thus not surprising that Zambia was unable to sustain its neo-orthodox adjustment efforts, which collapsed in May 1987. The "homegrown" adjustment program put together by the Zambians after the departure of the IMF and the World Bank clearly reflected the country's very scant technocratic and bureaucratic capabilities and the lack of political commitment to any form of neo-orthodox adjustment.

The Nigerian and Ghanaian Experiences

Although Nigeria's state capabilities are greater than those of Zambia, they are still weak by world standards. Because of intense domestic antipathy toward the IMF, the World Bank quietly played the central role in formulating Nigeria's structural adjustment program. During early 1986, Bank personnel worked directly with Nigerian officials grouped in an inter-ministerial committee established by the military regime. They also attempted to engage in extensive "policy dialogue" with influential members of the Nigerian elite. The resulting package was presented by General Ibrahim Babangida, Nigeria's military ruler, to his people as a "homespun" indigenous solution. It was then quietly formalized as an IMF stand-by agreement, although Nigeria did not plan to draw on the available funds. These were to be provided instead by the World Bank—again because of political sensitivities. Without its long-standing presence in Nigeria and the key background studies that it had already conducted, the Bank would not have been able to play this extraordinary role in helping Nigeria cope with its limited techno-cratic and bureaucratic capabilities and its strong internal political pressures. This effort was supported on the Nigerian side by a small but capable and stable economic team, decent political support and insula-tion by the military regime, and strong centralized authority.

In Ghana, the IMF and the World Bank jointly formulated adjust-ment strategy, in conjunction with a talented handful of economic offi-cials that had strong and consistent support from Jerry Rawlings, the country's military ruler. The result has been a remarkably sustained and successful economic recovery program since 1983—in fact the only major African story of economic reorientation. But despite the regime's political commitment to the reform effort and its success so far, the Gha-naian case illustrates other tensions inherent in the interdependent processes of conditionality and compensation for weak state capabili-ties.

One of the strengths of the reform effort in Ghana has been the quite strikingly stable involvement of the same senior officials in the reform process. But the pervasive administrative weakness of the Gha-naian state has greatly hampered policy formulation and, above all, implementation. Medium-term and long-term government planning has been almost nonexistent. Even basic data-gathering and analytical and accounting skills are rudimentary. The most effective reforms have been measures such as price changes, which do not involve continuous administrative action.

To compensate for administrative weakness, the economic recovery program has generated a real and quite visible resurgence of expatriate influence in Ghana—the nearly constant presence of IMF and World Bank personnel, visiting missions, hired consultants, and seconded bureaucrats and managers. The whole recovery effort is a high-condi-tionality process, and the Fund, the Bank, and the donor countries believe that expatriate personnel and their skills are necessary to ensure that their funds are used wisely. The World Bank, for example, sent more than forty missions to Ghana in 1987. Without much of this expatriate work, the adjustment effort would not have progressed nearly so far, but a real political problem has been created in the proc-ess. The often intense resentment of the role of expatriates has clearly identified the program with external actors and weakened its legiti-macy among key groups in Ghana. The long-term utility of expatriate involvement is also open to question unless it is supplemented by simultaneous and sustained training of nationals. These difficulties also affect Ghana's ability to absorb recently increased external financing prompted by the program's success to date.

Many African governments have themselves used expatriates—including individual advisors, investment banking groups, and law, public relations, accounting, and consulting firms—as part of their own bargaining strategy in the complicated, two-level "games" of adjustment. Such groups have been used most often for negotiating debt reschedulings, but also for devising strategies for dealing with the IMF and the World Bank. Many of the local economic and policy memoranda have in fact been written by foreign advisors. The long-term utility of these external efforts is also open to question.

Intense external involvement has generated another set of tensions. On the African side, Ghanaian officials complain about what they call the "macho policy school": The IMF, the World Bank, and the individual donor countries are always pushing, always desiring more in the way of change and conditionality. Once a change is made, they immediately want four more—and for the same amount of money. Speaking of the IMF in particular, Ghanaian officials ascribe this behavior to internal Fund politics in which officials concerned with their own careers want to "look tough" by leaning hard on African countries. Ghanaian officials argue that such relentless pressure jeopardizes the political and administrative viability of reform efforts. On the other side, officials from the Fund, the Bank, and the donor countries argue that if they do not push, the adjustment process will stall, especially since the reform efforts require simultaneous movement in multiple sectors. It is very difficult to find the precarious middle ground between these contending logics.

In countries with such weak capabilities, there is a clear link between task enormity, conditionality, adjustment fatigue, and sustainability. The huge, very time-consuming, and frustrating burdens of the adjustment process rest on the shoulders of a small group of people. They have to deal with a multitude of domestic groups and powerful international actors and their imposed conditionalities. "Burnout" and hasty, short-tempered responses to domestic opposition and external pressures can seriously jeopardize reform efforts.

A tension exists between sustainability and absorptive capacity. More resources are definitely needed to increase the chances for sustained reform, but due in large part to weak state capabilities, only so much can be absorbed effectively. Providing too many resources can undermine the economic foundations of the reform effort while reinforcing the political dynamics of rent-seeking. External actors have been hesitant to provide badly needed resources for a number of African countries due to the perception that they have weak state capabilities.

Such perceptions in turn reinforce the pressures for the use of expatriate personnel.

If new resources are to be used more effectively, some conditionality is necessary. If Zambia now illustrates African economic adjustment efforts in the absence of conditionality, Africa is in serious trouble. Conditionality is also an international fact of life and not likely to be avoided. But conditionality has gone wild. A need to coordinate, rationalize, target, and limit conditionality is clearly evident. Excessively detailed conditionality stimulates game-playing by both Third World and external officials, which in turn undermines the efficacy of reform and wastes the scarce resources committed to it. Rationalizing conditionality is, however, a difficult political as well as technical task. Time frame, pace, and sequencing are crucial matters to consider.

External efforts at "policy dialogue" and improving state capacity, as well as conditionality, can have quite unintended results when little or no political commitment to reform exists. In these cases, the outcome becomes the "ritual dances" of the adjustment game. Even long-term and sometimes intense IMF and World Bank involvement can produce very modest results. The interaction between external actors and the highly personalistic authoritarian regimes of Ferdinand Marcos in the Philippines and Mobutu Sese Seko in Zaire are classic examples of these "ritual dances."[18]

By 1981, the Philippines was involved in its sixteenth IMF program; the next year, 1982, was only the second since 1962 that the Marcos government did not participate in an IMF program. The results of this long-term supervision were modest at best. New institutions were created to rationalize and strengthen state capabilities, but they were soon transformed into window dressing by being captured, isolated, or ignored. The same has been true for the long series of agreements between Zaire and the IMF and the World Bank since the mid-1970s. In such predatory, rent-seeking states, agreements reached with technocratic officials do not reflect real commitment on the part of the regime; in fact, these officials are often used as political tools for dealing with external actors and legitimating the formal policies of a regime while contradictory political logics dominate actual practices. In 1981 and again in 1983, for example, the IMF discovered deliberate attempts by the Marcos government to deceive it in an effort to keep external assistance flowing. The 1983 crisis "revealed the extent to which the creditors had been lulled into complacency by the dualistic nature of the policy structure. The technocrats had not only proved impotent in controlling economic policy, they had also engaged in deception."[19] Effective technocratic capabilities actually declined during the course of the Marcos era as crony political logics dominated actual, as opposed to formal, policymaking.

Occasionally, out of sheer frustration, external actors have resorted to temporarily placing expatriates directly in key economic management positions. Such efforts in Zaire and Liberia failed to have any major impact, as the rent-seeking regimes simply circumvented the expatriate officials. External actors, particularly Western governments, should more consistently base financial support on action rather than announced policy, and they should reward those actually implementing difficult but necessary reforms regardless of their ideology or international political alignments. Mobutu Sese Seko of Zaire always talks reform, but carries through only briefly and opportunistically. Jerry Rawlings in Ghana, on the other hand, speaks in radical populist terms but has instituted the most successful and sustained neo-orthodox reform effort in Africa. Yet Western governments supported Mobutu while withholding important assistance from Rawlings during the fragile early phase of reform.[20] External actors need to be more selective in their support.

"Stop-go" cycles of reform are also facts of life, and external actors need to adjust to them more consistently and effectively. Such cycles can be linked to changing levels of ruler commitment to reform, to weak state capabilities, and to strong coalitional and societal pressures. Where little ruler commitment exists, and where the "ritual dances" of adjustment seem to predominate, as in Zaire and Liberia, the Fund, the Bank, and Western governments should be more inclined to pull out completely and stay out. This is now more politically feasible given Mikhail Gorbachev's stated intention to keep the Soviet Union out of costly new entanglements in the Third World. Even before Gorbachev's rise to power, the Soviets had told the new Rawlings regime in 1982 to go to the IMF and World Bank for help. Where ruler commitment exists or re-emerges, however, external actors should assiduously negotiate embedded liberal reform packages that are adequate to cope with the serious political, technical, and bureaucratic obstacles to change.

External pressure, influence, dialogue, and compensatory efforts are usually aimed at key political leaders, economic policymakers, technocrats, and top-level bureaucrats and do not extend to officials below these levels. This fact poses enormous difficulties for the sustained implementation of adjustment programs. The bureaucracy affects implementation in two ways: (1) through its administrative capabilities, and (2) through its role as an interest group and a channel for domestic as well as external pressures for particularistic attention.

Sheer administrative weakness can greatly threaten the effective implementation of an adjustment program. One striking example was the inability of the Zambian government over several years to collect bumper harvests of maize; ironically the good harvests reflected increased producer prices, which were part of the economic reform pack-

age. As recent World Bank data demonstrate, the elements of adjustment programs that have the highest rates of implementation are those
that do not require sustained administrative action.[21]

The bureaucracy is also an interest group, however. Neo-orthodox
adjustment programs not only have an anti-statist bias; they pose a
direct threat to specific interests of state officials at all levels. The
orthodox paradox raises its head here in very powerful ways. State officials can quietly undercut the effectiveness of reforms by not fully
implementing them or by providing "back-channel" input to non-state
actors, domestic and foreign, that want to blunt them. This has become
an increasingly important problem in Nigeria, where a threatened and
demoralized bureaucracy has been using its personalized discretion to
weaken reforms and to act as agents of powerful political groups jockey-
ing for power and position as the country approaches the return of democratic rule in 1992. Analysis of bureaucratic politics must disaggregate
the bureaucracy because adjustment policies bear differently on its various elements.

State Capability, Compensation, Embedded Liberalism, and Learning

One of the most common buzzwords used by external actors today when
discussing states with limited capabilities is "institution building."
Considerable thought and energy are going into increasing both governmental and private capabilities, so as to help both state and market
facilitate sustained neo-orthodox adjustment. These are important
efforts, but a little historical and institutional memory is in order. After
all, these problems are not new. For much of the 1960s and early 1970s,
the reigning catch-phrase was "development administration." It is
worth quoting one experienced and trenchant observer of "development
administration" in Africa at some length:

> The development administration movement did not survive
> long. . . . [It] was seen as a refinement of the bureaucratic mode of
> administration. It presupposed a "rational" bureaucracy in
> place. . . . The realities of the public service in the African countries
> after independence, [however], came quite soon to resemble the pat-
> rimonial [personalized] system with its tension between the invio-
> lability of tradition and the supremacy of sanctioned arbitrariness
> rather than the bureaucratic system with its tension between the
> equity of the rule and the equity of the case. Thus, the problem fac-
> ing the attempts to establish a "development administration" was
> not really the persistence but the disappearance of [colonial]
> bureaucratic norms and principles. With [personalized forms of

rule] taking over, the scope for administrative reform along the lines argued by local and expatriate professionals was severely reduced.

In order to understand the challenges of development management in Africa it is important not to start from the assumption that government services are overbureaucratized. Such a proposition is only correct if the definition of bureaucracy is confined to its negative characteristics—for example, excessive size and red tape—but such a view is not very helpful in terms of understanding the development tasks ahead . . . a proper time perspective is necessary. The development of a public service into a rational bureaucracy takes time . . . [P]umping more money into the state machinery and investing in manpower development programmes in present circumstances cannot be expected to make much of a difference unless certain conditions are met.[22]

As indicated at the beginning of this chapter, accelerating such historical trends as the shift from personalized to bureaucratic administration is very difficult indeed. No theory exists about how such shifts occur, much less about how to accelerate them.[23] Realistic expectations are in order; unrealistic optimism can lead to a backlash that might derail important but difficult efforts. The "fault of policy hurry" is just as damaging as the "fault of analytic hurry." The latter—the desire to rush things along whatever the path, to see things as real before they actually are, and to attribute exaggerated importance to social processes, institutions, and actors—has been very harmful to the study of current African realities. This has long been one of the major problems with the analysis of class factors in Africa. The same mistake could apply just as easily to institution building, the significance of informal economies, the spread and power of the market, or any of the other elements crucial to effective economic adjustment in the Third World. Neither academic analysts nor policymakers can unduly hasten or control social processes. Change is usually slow, incremental, uneven, often contradictory from a given analytical or policy point of view, and dependent on the outcome of unpredictable socioeconomic and political struggles. We cannot afford to stop looking for changes or trying to bring them about, but we must retain a sense of the historical complexity involved. The brutal death of the overly optimistic and voluntarist views of development so prevalent in the 1960s is but one pertinent example of the need to retain this perspective.

Some external actors have begun to learn important lessons relevant to increasing state capability and moving toward embedded liberalism in the Third World. These actors are those that have had the most day-to-day contact with the difficult dilemmas of economic adjustment: the World Bank, the IMF, and the aid agencies of the major Western governments. This is particularly true of the World Bank, as seen most vividly in its quite remarkable recent report entitled *Adjustment Lending: An Evaluation of Ten Years of Experience*. For example, in a section on "Institutional reform and Sub-Saharan Africa," the report notes that:

> The supply response to adjustment lending in low-income countries, especially in SSA has been slow because of the legacy of deep-seated structural problems. Inadequate infrastructure, poorly developed markets, rudimentary industrial sectors, and severe institutional and managerial weaknesses in the public and the private sectors have proved unexpectedly serious as constraints to better performance—especially in the poorer countries of SSA. Greater recognition thus needs to be given to the time and attention needed for structural changes, especially institutional reforms and their effects.[24]

Clearly the Bank now has a more realistic view of the complexities and difficulties of economic adjustment for countries with low levels of development, weak markets, and quite limited state capabilities.

Adjustment Lending calls for increased attention to the adequacy, speed, and timing of external finance; appropriate debt relief; buffering the social impact of adjustment on the urban and rural poor; and reducing the complexity and extent of conditionality. The report recognizes the need for swift and effective external actor coordination; proper pacing, timing, and sequencing of reforms; and sufficient time for appropriate institutional change. It also stresses the importance of tailoring adjustment programs to specific country contexts; suggests that more time be allotted for careful and expanded policy dialogue and consensus-building by all actors (that is, for more "government ownership" of reform programs); and recommends improving the quality of Bank advice through more systematic research, monitoring, and interaction with current and former economic and political officials. The report also recommends special allowances and flexibility for low-income countries, especially in the form of "greater sensitivity in the Bank to . . . the importance of nonprice factors in resource allocation." This requires an "emphasis on building institutions . . . given the need to implement and sustain policy reform over the longer term."[25] While these lessons are recognized by many people in the Bank, it is less clear that the Bank as an institution, especially one dependent on powerful Western countries, is prepared to translate these lessons into full-fledged policy.

Conclusions and Implications for Action

Important learning has taken place, and these new views have real policy implications for "monoeconomics," the orthodox paradox, the importance of a balanced tension between state and market and between economic and political logics, and the need for some form of embedded liberalism. The policy task at hand is to get these very important lessons translated into new policies and practice and to find the resources to back them up, with sufficient speed to make a real difference. In large part, this depends on domestic politics within Northern states as they define and pursue what they believe to be their interests, and on the linkage between Northern domestic politics and the organizational structure and politics of the IMF and the World Bank. Are these institutions truly committed to putting their newly acquired lessons into practice? And do they have the appropriate personnel, organizational structure, resources, and Western country support to do so?

What will it take to galvanize learning more fully: more close political calls such as the one in Mexico? More riots like those in Zambia, Venezuela, and Argentina? Will these lessons be applied mainly to countries perceived to be particularly important to the most powerful Northern states or more evenly and consistently on a case-by-case basis to countries that deserve special treatment based on commitment, severity of obstacles, and performance? Whether the Brady Plan, Japan's emerging role as an economic and political superpower, and recent new initiatives by the Fund and the Bank indicate a viable trend toward encouraging the development of embedded liberalism in the Third World remains to be seen.

It is not, however, just a question of the industialized world unilaterally reversing its attempt to bend Third World states to a pure form of economic liberalism that it does not apply to itself; rather, it is a question of both sides extending the compromise of embedded liberalism to the two-level games of economic adjustment. A serious attempt should be made to relink the domestic and international levels and economic and political logics in a more viable and sustained manner, with benefits accruing to all.[26] Such an effort requires continued learning by all actors in order to achieve and maintain the required delicately balanced tension between state and market and between political and economic logics. Embedded liberalism is an inherently unstable equilibrium, which can easily tip into unbalanced and unproductive statism on the one hand or the instabilities of unbridled market forces on the other. Maintaining this balance, and getting economic and political logics to reinforce rather than contradict each other, requires special state capabilities and sophisticated political and statecraft skills.

A driving force behind recent international learning is the increasingly palpable fear on the part of the IMF, the World Bank, and some elements of creditor-country governments that many of the economic reform programs currently under way in the Third World will fail completely unless fundamental changes are made. Speaking about Africa, a senior World Bank official has put this position honestly and bluntly:

> The alternative—a series of failed programs in Africa—is not worth thinking about, and not only because of the human suffering. . . . The basic idea of moving to a market economy, shifting policies out of grandiosity to step-by-step solid progress will be discredited. If they fail in a series of countries . . . then it is a failure of our approach to the economy, a failure of our institutions, a failure of our political will, and there's no way that we'll be able to say that it is just the failure of Africa! So we have a very, very big stake in this.[27]

To avoid such failure, Western governments need to allow all actors, but especially the IMF and the World Bank, the flexibility to experiment with ways to put the lessons they have learned during the last decade into practice *and* to provide the resources and debt relief required to make them work. This does not mean eliminating conditionality; rather, it means rationalizing it and making it more creatively flexible.

On the other side, a number of Third World leaders are beginning to realize that some movement toward neo-orthodox adjustment is imperative to avoid becoming increasingly marginalized in the rapidly changing world economy, with grave consequences for the long-term welfare of their peoples. Recent changes in the views of some Latin American leaders such as Michael Manley of Jamaica, Victor Paz Estenssoro of Bolivia, and Carlos Andrés Pérez of Venezuela are interesting in this regard. The Kwesi Botchweys of the Third World deserve help to more effectively work toward a balanced tension between state and market, to "maneuver [their] way around the naiveties of leftism . . . and the crudities and rigidities and dogma of monetarism."[28] Such learning and commitment, born of a recognition of Third World political and socioeconomic realities, need to be taken to heart by all actors in the two-level games of adjustment. The Botchweys need additional resources and increased state capabilities for any de facto attempt to move slowly and unevenly—but surely—toward a form of embedded liberalism, just as the industrialized economies have done in their own context for decades.

Several steps might facilitate a move toward embedded liberalism and increased state capability in the Third World:

1. Even Third World countries with considerable state capabilities, such as Mexico, require more rationalized and flexible forms of conditionality—ones that allow increased policy flexibility and resources to

help buffer the social and political costs of restructuring while sustaining the process.

2. External actors must learn to adjust more effectively and consistently to stop-go cycles of reform. When little leadership commitment exists, external actors, especially major Western governments, should be more inclined to pull out completely and stay out. When ruler commitment re-emerges, external actors should work hard to negotiate reform packages designed to cope with major obstacles. Zambia is a crucial test case at the moment. More viable forms of policy dialogue might facilitate learning on both sides that would assist a move toward embedded liberal compromises and fewer stop-go cycles.

3. For countries with limited state capabilities, a slower pace of adjustment and more sequencing of policy changes may be in order. The complex interrelationships between weak capability, task enormity, conditionality, adjustment fatigue, absorptive capacity, and sustainability need to be recognized and reflected in program design. The "macho policy" attitudes of external agencies are distinctly counterproductive in this regard. Obstacles to adjustment are much greater and more complex than a mere lack of political will or even of coalitional support. An announcement of policy and institutional changes does not mean that such changes will actually take place, even under the best of conditions.

4. More care and sensitivity in the use of expatriate personnel is necessary so that their very presence does not catalyze opposition—weakening the legitimacy and viability of reform efforts. The use of expatriates should be combined with the utilization and training of available local personnel wherever possible. In some circumstances, the "twinning" of expatriate experts with local personnel may help mitigate some of the tension while working to improve local capabilities. In light of the experiences of Zaire and Liberia, however, direct takeovers of local institutions should be avoided, as these do not achieve the desired results.

5. It is very difficult to "build" state capacity as part of a perceived policy imperative. Nevertheless, it is important that efforts to improve state capabilities be undertaken. As experience illustrates, however, engaging in "institution-building" and attempts to overcome other political and social obstacles to adjustment require modest expectations and steady and consistent effort over a considerable period of time. Major pushes and shifting from one fad approach to another only produce cynicism and disappointment when the results are meager or the programs stopped.

In short, in a world where the Chinese government has recently confronted powerful political implications of its impressive economic reforms and the Soviets are attempting to implement *perestroika,* we need to help the Third World do what we have done all along, not what we have been preaching all along. But whether these necessities become possibilities or not depends on how all actors define and pursue their interests, and on the outcome of the struggles waged over them.

Notes

[1] "Ghana: High Stakes Gamble," *Africa News,* Vol. 31, No. 2 (23 January 1989), p. 10.

[2] See Miles Kahler, "Orthodoxy and Its Alternatives: Explaining Approaches to Stabilization and Adjustment," in Joan M. Nelson, ed., *Economic Crisis and Policy Choice: The Politics of Economic Adjustment in the Third World* (Princeton, N.J.: Princeton University Press, forthcoming 1990).

[3] Max Weber, *General Economic History* (New Brunswick, N.J.: Transaction Books, 1981), and *Economy and Society* (Berkeley: University of California Press, 1978); Randall Collins, "Weber's Last Theory of Capitalism," *American Sociological Review,* Vol. 45 (December 1980), pp. 925–42; Karl Polanyi, *The Great Transformation* (New York: Rinehart, 1944); Alexander Gerschenkron, *Economic Backwardness in Historical Perspective* (Cambridge, Mass.: Harvard University Press, 1962); Douglass C. North and Robert Paul Thomas, *The Rise of the Western World: A New Economic History* (Cambridge: Cambridge University Press, 1973); Douglass C. North, *Structure and Change in Economic History* (New York: Norton, 1981); Albert O. Hirschman, *The Passions and the Interests: Political Arguments for Capitalism Before Its Triumph* (Princeton, N.J.: Princeton University Press, 1977); Thomas M. Callaghy, "The State and the Development of Capitalism in Africa: Theoretical, Historical, and Comparative Reflections," in Donald Rothchild and Naomi Chazan, eds., *The Precarious Balance: State and Society in Africa* (Boulder, Colo.: Westview Press, 1988), pp. 67–99.

[4] Dietrich Rueschemeyer and Peter B. Evans, "The State and Economic Transformation: Toward an Analysis of the Conditions Underlying Effective Intervention," in P. B. Evans, D. Rueschemeyer, and T. Skocpol, eds., *Bringing the State Back In* (New York: Cambridge University Press, 1985), pp. 51, 71.

[5] Ibid., pp. 49, 51.

[6] Kenneth N. Waltz, *Theory of International Politics* (Reading, Mass.: Addison-Wesley Publishing Co., 1979), p. 109.

[7] On East Asia, see Stephan Haggard and Chung-in Moon, "The South Korean State in the International Economy: Liberal, Dependent, or Mercantile?" in John Gerard Ruggie, *The Antinomies of Interdependence* (New York: Columbia University Press, 1983), pp. 131–89; Alice H. Amsden, "The State and Taiwan's Economic Development," in Evans et al., *Bringing the State Back In,* op. cit., pp. 78–106; and Frederic C. Deyo, ed., *The Political Economy of the New Asian Industrialism* (Ithaca, N.Y.: Cornell University Press, 1987). On Latin America, see Peter B. Evans, "Class, State and Dependence in East Asia: Lessons for Latin Americanists," in Deyo, *Political Economy,* op. cit., pp. 203–26, and *Dependent Development: The Alliance of Multinational, State and Local Capital in Brazil* (Princeton, N.J.: Princeton University Press, 1979).

[8] Stephan Haggard and Robert Kaufman, "The Politics of Stabilization and Structural Adjustment," in Jeffrey D. Sachs, ed., *Developing Country Debt and Economic Performance,* Vol. 1, *The International System* (Chicago: University of Chicago Press, 1989), p. 246.

[9] The term and concept are John Gerard Ruggie's; see his "International Regimes, Transactions and Change: Embedded Liberalism in the Postwar Economic Order," *International Organization,* Vol. 36, No. 2 (Spring 1982), especially pp. 398–99, 405, 413. Robert Gilpin and Barry Buzan both prefer the term "benign mercantilism"; see Robert Gilpin, *The Political Economy of International Relations* (Princeton, N.J.: Princeton University Press, 1987), pp. 404–5. I prefer "embedded liberalism" because it more accurately reflects the direction of policy change and the balancing point between state and market.

[10] See John Gerard Ruggie, "Political Structure and Change in the International Economic Order: The North–South Dimension," in Ruggie, *The Antinomies of Interdependence,* op. cit., pp. 423–87.

[11] On two-level games, see Robert D. Putnam, "Diplomacy and Domestic Politics: The

Logic of Two-level Games," *International Organization*, Vol. 42, No. 3 (Summer 1988), pp. 427–60.

[12] World Bank, *Adjustment Lending: An Evaluation of Ten Years of Experience* (Washington, D.C.: The World Bank, 1988), p. 65; this observation obviously needs to be disaggregated by country, but this rough cut is sufficient for the purposes of this analysis.

[13] See Barbara Stallings, "Politics and Economic Crisis: A Comparative Study of Chile, Peru, and Colombia," in Nelson, ed., *Economic Crisis and Policy Choice* op. cit.

[14] Ibid.

[15] Ibid.

[16] See Robert Kaufman, "Stabilization and Adjustment in Argentina, Brazil, and Mexico," in Nelson, ed., *Economic Crisis and Policy Choice*, op. cit.

[17] See Thomas M. Callaghy, "Lost Between State and Market: The Politics of Economic Adjustment in Ghana, Zambia, and Nigeria," in Nelson, ed., *Economic Crisis and Policy Choice*, op. cit.

[18] See Stephan Haggard, "The Political Economy of the Philippine Debt Crisis," in Nelson, ed., *Economic Crisis and Policy Choice*, op. cit.; and Thomas M. Callaghy, "The Political Economy of African Debt: The Case of Zaire," in John Ravenhill, ed., *Africa in Economic Crisis* (New York: Columbia University Press, 1986), pp. 307–46.

[19] Haggard, "The Politics of the Philippine Debt Crisis," op. cit.

[20] The U.S. government has recently provided a vivid example of this problem. In early 1989, the U.S. Agency for International Development (USAID) revised its categories for allocating resources from the Development Fund for Africa. In the new classification, political criteria were to be downplayed and developmental standards weighted more heavily. The highest category was to include countries with a demonstrated commitment to sound and/or improved economic policies, good potential for economic growth, capability for managing serious debt or foreign exchange problems, and a population over seven million. USAID's new "top ten" category includes both Ghana and Zaire. Clearly the latter does not belong on this list. The other eight countries on the list are: Senegal, Mali, Guinea, Cameroon, Uganda, Kenya, Malawi, and Madagascar.

[21] World Bank, *Adjustment Lending*, op. cit.

[22] Goran Hyden, *No Shortcuts to Progress* (Berkeley: University of California Press, 1983), pp. 76, 77, 78–79.

[23] This is a real research frontier for analysts concerned with policy and academics interested in comparative historical sociology. See Thomas M. Callaghy, "The State and the Development of Capitalism in Africa," op. cit.; and *The State-Society Struggle* (New York: Columbia University Press, 1984).

[24] World Bank, *Adjustment Lending*, op. cit., p. 3.

[25] Ibid., p. 65.

[26] The international relations literature is now stressing this linkage; see Stephan Haggard and Beth Simmons, "Theories of International Regimes," *International Organization*, Vol. 41, No. 3 (Summer 1987), pp. 491–517; and Putnam, "Diplomacy and Domestic Politics," op. cit.

[27] Margaret A. Novicki, "Interview with Edward V. K. Jaycox, Vice-President, Africa Region, The World Bank," *Africa Report*, Vol. 32, No. 6 (November–December 1987), p. 32.

[28] "Ghana: High Stakes Gamble," *Africa News*, op. cit., p. 10.

Chapter 6

International Financial Institutions and the Politics of Adjustment

Miles Kahler

Conditionality—or the economic policy changes that external agencies require of national governments in the course of adjustment—remains a source of political contention both between governments and their creditors and in the domestic politics of individual countries. Part of the conflict between international financial institutions (IFIs) and developing-country governments may simply emerge from the position of the IFIs at the center of a creditor coalition and their association with economic outcomes that in many of these countries have been mediocre or worse. Nevertheless, conflict over conditionality has appeared during periods of strong economic performance, such as the late 1950s and 1960s, as well as those of economic stagnation, such as the 1980s. The persistence of such contention suggests that its roots may be political and that better economic outcomes may require dealing with its political sources. Attention to the politics of adjustment points to strategies for reducing, if not eliminating, these sources of conflict. Those strategies—notably greater reliance on policy dialogue and the provision of higher levels of financing—in turn have political prerequisites that require attention.

Models of Conditionality

For commercial banks and other private creditors, intervention in the politics of adjustment is driven by a desire for repayment, which requires oversight of the economic policies that are central to any government's economic strategy and political standing. For multilateral, public financial institutions—the International Monetary Fund (IMF) and the World Bank will be of principal concern in this discussion—repayment is neither the beginning nor the end of their involvement; their impetus for oversight is broader. The Fund does emphasize the need for prompt repayment to ensure the revolving, short-term nature of Fund resources. In the case of the Bank, the term of lending is less significant than the basis of the Bank's financing in the confidence of the private financial markets—in contrast to the Fund's reliance on the subscriptions of its members. More important to both institutions, however, is their interest in national policies that impinge on central responsibilities assigned to them by their members. For the IMF, those responsibilities include surveillance of exchange rate policies (and by extension, macroeconomic policies) and ensuring that the adjustment policies chosen do not conflict with other purposes of the organization, such as a liberalized trade and payments system and the promotion of economic growth. The Bank, with its goals of economic development and poverty alleviation, has become increasingly concerned about the need for a stable economic environment in which to carry on its traditional project lending. The international economic shocks of the 1970s and 1980s provided an additional stimulus to the development of structural adjustment and sectoral lending with policy conditions.[1]

Official rhetoric at the Fund and the Bank often emphasizes that relations with borrowing governments are apolitical, consensual, and non-interventionist: Programs are designed by governments to meet their own needs; if they also meet the IMF and World Bank criteria, then they will be supported financially. In the words of one experienced World Bank staff member:

> the word *leverage* does not occur in the Bank's lexicon ... the Bank's policy assistance has been essentially a cooperative venture with the recipient countries. Successful country programs must be homegrown and cannot be standardized or externally imposed; they should be designed and perceived as central to the countries' own interests. The Bank plays a supplemental role, backing up and helping to implement sound policy initiatives.[2]

An alternative view that emphasizes the coercive element in conditionality pervades statements by developing-country governments. Paul Mosley has elaborated this model of bargaining between national governments and Bretton Woods institutions, positing an underlying conflict of interest: The borrowing country would prefer to take the money and run, gaining financial relief with few policy changes; the external agency, meanwhile, is intent on ensuring that finance accompanies (or even follows) only desired policy changes.[3] Mosley's model of bargaining assumes that pressures for deviation from conditions imposed by lenders arise in domestic politics. External agencies ask for policy changes that may impose political risks (since economic recovery may not coincide with political tests such as elections) and political costs (because of the differing incidence of policy changes on different members of political coalitions).

Both of these stylized models—the harmonious image of the Fund and the Bank or the more coercive portrait of their critics—fall short of incorporating the politics of adjustment in their assessments of conditionality. Although IMF and World Bank staff are often keenly aware of political divisions within countries and take those divisions into account in their bargaining stance, the organizations officially have lapsed too frequently into calls for "political will" or "political courage"—coming close to reducing the politics of adjustment to an exercise in *machismo.* For different reasons, developing-country governments and critics of the IFIs do not wish to encourage closer outside scrutiny of and intervention in local politics. Instead, conflicts are often elevated to an ideological plane that may be the least important feature of domestic resistance to an adjustment program.

Both models assume unitary political actors—typically the IMF or the World Bank on one side and a government in need of external finance on the other. In fact, neither portrait is particularly accurate in the 1980s. The Fund and the Bank have become closely associated with creditor coalitions that include aid donors and official creditors among the industrialized countries as well as private creditors (typically commercial banks). The need for coordination among these creditors—and the possibilities of overt conflict among them—change the relationship between debtor governments and external agencies. Divisions within the creditor coalition also provide the opening for reverse leverage exerted by the borrowing country: A shrewd political elite can play upon rifts between IFIs and creditor governments to weaken conditionality and to obtain higher levels of finance.

As accounts of the politics of adjustment demonstrate, a unitary image rarely fits a beleaguered government confronting difficult economic decisions during adjustment. Divided and sometimes paralyzed, politicians and technocrats contend for influence over the instruments of policy. Debtor-country governments facing a creditor coalition are themselves often coalitions—a fact that external agencies can use to their advantage in bargaining. Such internal divisions therefore are not likely to be emphasized by governments, however critical they are of conditionality.

Moreover, even unified governments rarely reflect a unified society. They must bargain at two tables simultaneously, managing their financing strategy vis-à-vis external creditors so that the outcome in the external game is politically sustainable in the domestic political game.[4]

The payoffs or penalties in the first game—those offered or threatened by the Fund, the Bank, or private external creditors—may need to be recalculated when outcomes feed into domestic political contests. As Paul Mosley and many others have suggested, the opposition of domestic interest groups is one important explanation for the defection of governments from agreements on policy changes.

The political conflict surrounding adjustment—between external agencies and debtor governments, within governments, and between governments and groups in their societies—can erupt in three areas. First, the *content of the programs* and even the model of how the economy works may be at issue. Much of the debate over conditionality has centered on this question: Do the IMF and the World Bank have the right policy prescriptions for a particular society? Nevertheless, ideological divisions—or arguments over principle, as Richard Cooper has termed them—seem to have diminished in the 1980s.[5] Heterodox challenges to the Fund have focused less on different models of developing economies than on judgments about particular economies, on the relative weight to be assigned to goals other than balance-of-payments adjustment (such as growth or equity), and on the malleability of the international environment. Although convergence has occurred in the 1980s on macroeconomic policy prescriptions—a result of changes in both the IFIs and the developing countries—structural adjustment measures, with their deeper institutional implications, still inspire debate.

A second and more significant source of political conflict has been *nationalist resentment* of the external intervention implied by conditionality. Particularly when managed in an intrusive way, the imposition and monitoring of economic policies can lead to strong pressures from groups inside as well as outside government to shake off those constraints. Governments will seek to preserve their policymaking autonomy against external directives; the appearance of subordination to such directives may lower their legitimacy and therefore their ability to implement chosen policies.

Finally, conditionality and the policy changes it entails affect *the economic interests and political standing of groups inside and outside government* in different ways. One prediction is a certainty: Some will perceive themselves as losers in the process and will react to that threat of loss. Government employees resist layoffs and pay freezes; politicians oppose the dismantling of state enterprises that provide them with patronage; import-competing industries argue against trade liberalization. If these changes are coupled with economic stagnation, the list of losers grows longer.[6]

Each of these aspects of domestic political conflict surrounding conditionality and adjustment interacts with three different dimensions of the role of external agencies. First, *policy conditions* themselves may cover wider or narrower areas of economic policy; conditionality undoubtedly has been made more difficult and more politically contentious by greater emphasis on structural adjustment measures such as trade liberalization or the reform of public sector enterprises. The timing of the changes—gradualist or "shock treatment"—has long been controversial. In addition, conditions may be waived in the breach; this is one measure of the tightness of conditionality.

Second, on the basis of their policy conditions, international financial institutions generate *financing,* both directly and from other sources that they are able to mobilize. If conditionality arouses political resistance of several varieties, finance may offer one means for lowering opposition by slowing the pace of adjustment, maintaining levels of economic growth, and permitting the compensation of losers in the adjustment process. Of course, easing the political pain of adjustment may also lead to avoiding difficult economic decisions altogether. Many of the strategies pursued by external agencies have been attempts to support adjustment measures without offering incentives for deviating from a politically difficult course.

The third dimension of external involvement in adjustment—the degree of oversight and detailed monitoring of the implementation of conditionality—has been particularly significant in countries where administrative capabilities are weak. For larger countries with a substantial technocratic core, bargaining over the shape of an adjustment program involves weighing the domestic political costs attached to changing a particular policy course against the benefits of an infusion of finance. Smaller countries with a narrower administrative base must also calculate the political costs of an intrusive external presence in designing and implementing the program.

These elements of conditionality have been much analyzed and criticized, with particular attention to the coherence and appropriateness of the economic programs promoted. There has not been much analysis, however, of the interactions between conditionality and the politics of adjustment. Conditionality coupled with financing might increase the probability that a particular adjustment program will be adopted and implemented, but the precise mechanisms through which the politics of adjustment are tilted by such intervention have remained relatively obscure.[7] Have the Fund and the Bank—through their intervention in the politics of adjustment—made the government's task even harder? Could better management of their perceived or actual participation in the politics of adjustment have produced better outcomes—both in the economic welfare of the developing countries and in their own standing and future relations with those countries? Before addressing this question, we must consider a logically prior issue: Have external agencies and their conditionality actually made much difference—for better or worse—in stabilization and adjustment outcomes?

What Difference Does Conditionality Make?

Although the Fund and the Bank argue that they offer financial support to programs already "owned" by governments, their elaboration of conditionality appears to be designed to counter the threat of defection from these supposedly self-imposed programs. In the case of the IMF, if a government is known to have derailed programs in the past, preconditions may be required before Executive Board approval of a stand-by or extended arrangement is granted. Fund programs and most policy-based Bank loans (structural adjustment and sectoral adjustment loans) disburse their program financing in tranches, as a further deterrent to slippage from agreed policy changes. In the case of the Fund, those disbursements are dependent on performance criteria, particular macroeconomic targets, and satisfactory review of the program by Fund staff. The structure of Bank conditionality is somewhat similar, with short-term, specific actions embedded in a program of medium-term (five to seven years) and broader targets.

Two features of this structure point toward skepticism about its effectiveness in inducing policy change (assuming some conflict over the program's content and timing). First, conditionality is not rigidly applied, and countries realize that it is not: Waivers can be granted if programs go off track; programs may be cancelled, but negotiations for new programs often begin soon after. The larger and more strategically or symbolically important the country, the less likely that it will be indefinitely cut off from the use of IMF or World Bank resources.

A second and more recent development is the widened scope of conditionality. Instead of a few macroeconomic targets, conditionality —particularly in World Bank structural adjustment lending—has been broadened to include measures of policy reform that are far more difficult to monitor. Two effects of this broadening have weakened the existing model of conditionality. As programs become broader, performance may vary widely across the measures incorporated in the program. If a country receives mixed grades on its program—high marks in one area and failing marks in another—the overall judgment of its performance becomes blurred and the sanction of program termination is unlikely to be employed.[8] As Paul Mosley suggests, evaluation is also rendered difficult, if not impossible, by the long lags between commitment and implementation under the new and broader definition of conditionality. It may take years to detect failure.[9]

Early scholarly attempts to measure the effects of Fund or Bank conditionality (like many popular and journalistic efforts today) concentrated on the *economic* effects of those programs and made simple "before-and-after" comparisons: Did economic performance improve by some measure after acceptance of a Fund stand-by or a World Bank structural adjustment loan? As John Williamson has pointed out, this standard is clearly biased against the international financial institutions, since it assumes that the prior economic trajectory could be sustained in the absence of policy changes urged by the external agencies.[10]

If such a standard of comparison is dismissed, however, measurement becomes a series of complicated comparisons of "what might have been" that can only be addressed through a careful examination of cases. The principal influence of the IFIs on economic outcomes is their ability to alter the economic policy trajectory of a country. Two further influences, suggested by Morris Goldstein and Peter Montiel, may flow from the IFIs' encouragement of policy change: IMF or World Bank support for a program may increase the overall level of confidence in the country's economy, affecting public and private capital inflows in particular; likewise, an economic program supported by external agencies may also increase the effectiveness of any given policy change by altering the expectations of local business or other agents in the economy.[11]

In assessing the impact of external agents and conditionality on governmental decisions to undertake and implement programs of adjustment, one returns to the core issue of the politics of adjustment. Indeed, the influence of external agencies on political decisions to undertake one economic program rather than another, to act rather than to delay, are important prior assessments needed for determining (a) whether those programs, if undertaken, would produce an economic outcome better than that which would have ensued in the absence of external conditionality and finance; and (b) whether another set of policies that might have produced an even better outcome was ignored by the Fund and the Bank.[12] This second set of questions concerns the economic model that the IMF and the World Bank endorse and the issue of whether it is the best model for particular countries or developing countries more generally. It is important to emphasize, however, that disputes over the model must first demonstrate that the model is implementable, at least in some rough form, in the countries under examination.

Bringing the politics of adjustment to an examination of the effectiveness of conditionality, however, raises once again the question of the appropriateness of Fund and Bank prescriptions by the back door. As noted above, political contention over the content of policy advice is one of the reasons that external conditionality is controversial in developing countries. Nationalist reactions are another. The political explosions that may surround the entry of the IMF or the World Bank into the adjustment process may convince some governments that undertaking such a program is not worth the risk. Studies of Fund and Bank programs carried out from the perspective of economics are careful to take into account the biased sample represented by those countries undertaking IMF or World Bank programs: They may represent a set of cases with worse economic prospects than the larger group of developing countries. The sample may be biased in another way, however, in that some countries may choose *not* to come to the international financial institutions simply because of the political consequences that they fear will result from such a step; several Latin American countries, including Brazil and Venezuela, have fallen into this category. Another important point is raised in these cases as well: Would they have pursued economic policies that produced better outcomes with access to the economic policy advice and, most important, the finance that could be mobilized by the IFIs? That alternative was often ruled out because of political resistance to involvement by the IFIs.

Similar reasoning points to a second set of countries that are important in assessing the role of conditionality and external agencies: those countries that seemed to undertake their change of course without the intervention of the IMF or the World Bank. For these countries —Chile, Mexico, and Turkey are possible examples—external conditionality was not important, although financial support may have been.

Studies of the effects of conditionality that have examined the first—and most political—question of whether policy trajectories change under external influence point to a record of mixed implementation at best. Tony Killick's review of IMF programs, based on IMF program data and case studies, suggests that "the Fund has experienced considerable difficulty in ensuring that its programmes are implemented." As Killick notes, the IMF itself has assigned a large measure of the failure to implement to "political constraints" and "weak administrative systems."[13] Stephan Haggard's study of Extended Fund Facility agreements with the IMF also points out a dismal record of implementation. Of the thirty cases studied, twenty-four were not implemented in their original form; sixteen were cancelled.[14] In a study of African adjustment programs supported by the IMF in 1980–81, the record in reducing the fiscal deficit and restraining the growth of net domestic credit was found to be poor. Most countries failed to achieve their fiscal target, and only about half reached their credit objectives.[15]

The record of World Bank policy-based lending appears to be equally mixed if the criterion applied is the full implementation of the conditions attached to the loans. A recent study of structural adjustment loans (SALs) and sector adjustment loans (SECALs) in fifteen developing countries shows an overall compliance rate of about 60 per cent. The record rises to 80 per cent if "substantial progress" rather than full compliance on conditions is the criterion. One trend that clearly emerges is variation across policy areas: The manipulation of prices generally meets with greater success, and those areas that are not politically sensitive and do not require institution-building also display relatively higher compliance.[16]

A recent set of case studies on the politics of stabilization and structural change in developing countries has attempted to estimate the independent effects of external agencies on government decisions to undertake stabilization or broader structural adjustment programs and on government implementation of those programs. The study divided the programs into two sets—those that stopped at stabilization measures and those that carried out a broader program of policy change, whether orthodox or heterodox.[17]

In general, external agencies exercised significant influence on decisions to undertake stabilization programs (uniformly of an orthodox variety) on governments of a particular political configuration. On the one hand, a number of deeply divided or paralyzed governments could not be pushed into such programs despite clear external pressure; their internal political authority had eroded, and domestic resistance was calculated to be too great. At the other end of the spectrum, a number of governments—including Chile under Augusto Pinochet, Mexico under Miguel de la Madrid, and Costa Rica under Alberto Monge—had clearly decided upon a program of economic adjustment before commitment of external finance or the involvement of external advisors. External backing for orthodox choices probably reinforced that course, but it is difficult to argue that external agencies determined either the timing or the scope of decisions in these cases.

In only a few, delicately balanced cases did external agencies seem to tilt decisions on economic programs in favor of stabilization. The Philippines under Ferdinand Marcos in late 1984, the Dominican Republic under Jorge Blanco, also in 1984, and Zambia under Kenneth Kaunda in 1985 were divided regimes, and for them the Bretton Woods institutions represented the lenders of last resort. In Ghana in 1982–83, after years of economic disaster, the need for external finance reinforced the arguments of a coherent economic team that initiated and then broadened an orthodox stabilization and adjustment program.[18] Even in these cases, in which the external agencies were able to forge a temporary alliance with only one part of the government (comparable to the much-discussed British case of 1976), the outcomes were decidedly mixed. Zambia's stabilization ended in May 1987 with defiance of the International Monetary Fund; an increasingly isolated Kenneth Kaunda and a small economic team could not surmount the organized interests—political and economic—that resisted the program. In the Dominican Republic, the Jorge Blanco government was able to institute some tough stabilization measures in 1984–85, but there was little hint of any political interest in broader structural reforms; by 1989, even the transient gains of stabilization had been eroded by the successor government of Joaquín Balaguer.

The Marcos government in the Philippines also implemented stabilization measures urged by the international financial institutions and the U.S. government in 1984, but the program failed to move beyond stabilization. The Marcos case is particularly interesting, since it seems to confirm a conventional bargaining view of IMF/Bank relations with national governments. Loose conditionality in the 1970s, coupled with widened access to commercial bank loans, permitted Marcos to perpetuate the existing structure of crony capitalism. After the assassination of Benigno Aquino, closer coordination of lending by the IMF and the World Bank and a tightening of conditionality (following the discovery that the Philippines central bank had doctored its books), led to intensified external pressure on Marcos for tough stabilization measures. The reinforced conditionality was, however, undercut by three features of the situation: the softer line endorsed by the United States, indicating a lack of creditor coordination; the electoral cycles of a transitional regime; and, perhaps most important, Marcos's ability to shield politically sensitive areas of policymaking from both external and technocratic scrutiny.[19] In each of these cases of divided and hesitant regimes, external agencies were able to press governments toward enacting stabilization programs, but those programs did not extend beyond short-term measures to rectify balance-of-payments deficits.

In the cases studied, the IMF and the World Bank were deeply involved in implementing both stabilization and neo-orthodox structural adjustment programs. Their involvement grew in smaller countries—particularly those with limited state capabilities, where the technocratic team was stretched to the limit. Ghana, Jamaica, and Zambia offer clear examples of such intervention in implementation. One Zambian official remarked that "the IMF and the World Bank have become the Ministry of Finance in Zambia."[20] Overall, however, any connection between deeper involvement by external agencies and success in implementation is difficult to discern in these cases. In the Philippines, for example, IMF and World Bank involvement in structural adjustment had been persistent since the 1970s. But the government of Corazon Aquino was able to move ahead with a partial program of economic reforms that Marcos had failed to implement. Domestic political parameters—not the level of World Bank involvement—had changed. The Aquino government was able to overcome resistance to the reforms in part by portraying them as a break with the Marcos era and an attack on crony capitalism.[21]

The historical record, in short, suggests that external agencies exercise limited influence on decisions to adopt stabilization and structural adjustment programs and on their successful implementation. One plausible counter to this preliminary finding is that alternative sources of finance in the 1970s and early 1980s undercut the leverage of the international financial institutions; drastic limits on commercial bank lending after 1982 increased the possibilities for external influence. But the studies cited above, while often demonstrating the importance of a heightened financial constraint, do not reveal a consistent pattern of greater influence in the 1980s. A recent study of Latin American programs that extends to 1984 argues that the power of the Bretton Woods institutions has been inflated:

> To describe the IMF as a "poverty broker," as does the title of a recent book, or to charge the Fund with undermining democracy is to engage in hyperbole. The power of the IMF remains a useful myth for governments seeking a scapegoat to explain difficult economic conditions associated with severe balance-of-payments disequilibria, but the ability of the IMF to impose programs from the outside is distinctly limited.[22]

An analysis based on the politics of adjustment seems to confirm this judgment. Both the spokesmen of the IMF and the World Bank and their critics in academia and the developing countries have been engaged in a lengthy debate that seems based on a faulty estimate of external influence over the process of adjustment. Perhaps, however, this debate is not simply sound and fury. Perhaps different programs, arrived at by a different and less politically charged route, would produce a better record of implementation and more desirable economic outcomes from the points of view of both the IFIs and developing countries. That hope is embodied in the revival of interest in policy dialogue, which risks being seen as a panacea for the political obstacles to policy change that have been apparent in the 1980s.

The Renewal of Dialogue and the Politics of Adjustment

The apparent inefficacy of tight conditionality lends support to the chorus of observers who argue for a different model of Fund and Bank relations with developing countries—one less dependent upon refined stipulations of policy change leveraged through access to finance and more dependent on persuasion, dialogue, and joint problem-solving. The elites of developing countries have long complained of the tutelary attitude of the IMF and the World Bank. A gathering of African central bank governors and technocrats—typically the allies within their governments of the IFIs—complained of their encounters with IMF staff:

Many, including some with reasonably successful Fund programs, suggested that the Fund staff is inadequately informed or insensitive with respect to local conditions and objectives, patronizing in their relationships with local professionals, and rigid or powerless or both in their negotiations with African governments.[23]

Despite a tradition of policy dialogue at the World Bank, structural adjustment loans have also been criticized for failing to promote "effective dialogue, the fashioning of a true meeting of minds on policy issues. . . . The SAL process permits little genuine dialogue between believers (Bank and local) and non-believers—local technicians and political leaders who doubt the applicability and/or efficacy of the Bank's medicine."[24] Gerald K. Helleiner has argued that "dialogue rather than arm-twisting is the appropriate mode for Bank-member interaction."[25] In effect, both insiders and outside critics argue that the official view of conditionality—as support for a mutually acceptable program rather than a coercive process of bargaining—should be the model of relations between developing countries and the IFIs.

The atmosphere of crisis that has surrounded many Fund programs since 1982 has been a serious obstacle to a more reflective and symmetrical process of program design. The need to reach agreements quickly and begin disbursements—for reasons of system stability in the case of the larger debtor countries—has often telescoped or undermined the course of policy dialogue. On the other hand, if the lending operations of the Fund and the Bank could be more deeply embedded in continuous policy consultations with national authorities, the need for crisis lending could be alleviated in the future. Stand-bys might become actual stand-bys—that is, credit lines available to governments that they might choose *not* to utilize—and negotiations over IMF and Bank programs would become only one dimension of a broader and longer set of discussions.

The framework for such an alternative has been in place for some time in the form of Article IV consultations with the IMF and policy dialogue with the World Bank, and it has worked quite well in some cases. Consider, for example, remarks by the Minister of Finance of Korea on the occasion of the closing of the IMF Resident Representative office in Seoul in July 1987, after twenty-two years of continuous operation:

The annual consultation discussions between the Korean Government and the IMF have also been a guiding influence over the Korean economy. . . . The result has been a richer menu of policy options. . . . In day-to-day contacts with officials at all levels in the various economic ministries, the IMF Resident Representative gained a unique understanding of the Korean economy. This broad-based understanding no doubt contributed greatly toward promoting a deeper appreciation in the IMF, as well as other financial institutions abroad, of Korean economic policies and the specific constraints we face.[26]

The contrast between the Asian experience and that of many Latin American and African countries is stark. In assessing the cost to Brazil of not turning to the IMF in 1979–80, Carlos Díaz-Alejandro remarked that "the resulting high cost is not a measure of their irrationality, but an appalling indictment of the Fund's record over the past 35 years in dealing with Brazil."[27] The World Bank may arouse less sensitivity and achieve more success in its policy dialogues, but its coupling with the IMF as one of the "terrible twins" in much African discussion suggests that the Bank has not escaped a similar reputation. Such variation in the success of dialogue across countries raises the possibility that national politics explains part of the record. An examination of the interaction of the politics of adjustment and the course of dialogue could produce suggestions for increasing commitment to dialogue on both sides and to improving the uneven record of program implementation.

The value of dialogue in increasing government commitment to an economic program lies primarily in its effect on the three sources of political resistance. By heightening the probability of more symmetrical negotiations, dialogue lowers opposition that springs from disagreement over the underlying model of the economy. In avoiding the appearance of policy dictation by the IMF or the World Bank, nationalist distrust of external agencies can also be reduced. Routinizing and extending consultations could reduce the political sensitivity of negotiations over Fund and Bank lending. Finally, if dialogue does not lower the resistance of economic interests adversely affected by adjustment, it might, through closer consultations with governments, make IFIs more sensitive to those voices of dissent when formulating policy advice. Overall, such discussions lengthen the "shadow of the future"—the realization on the part of both IFIs and governments that they will confront one another in the context of such discussions at regular intervals. Crisis-determined lending, on the other hand, offers no such assurance.

Despite widespread agreement on the value of reviving continuous policy dialogue in place of intermittent lending at times of external crisis, little attention has been given to the political prerequisites and pitfalls of dialogue for both sides. The IMF and the World Bank must be willing to discuss alternative diagnoses and to experiment with heterodox programs if such an approach is to succeed. Cautious IMF support for Argentina's Austral Plan and the recent creation by the Fund of a Compensatory and Contingency Financing Facility (CCFF) suggest that developing-country initiatives have begun to find expression in official policy.[28] A second caution for the IFIs concerns coordination of conditionality within the creditor coalition. If the IMF and the World Bank develop joint positions in their negotiations with national governments, they may introduce a new element of rigidity into those discussions, hindering the evolution of dialogue. The IMF and the World Bank may also need to distance themselves from private creditors in dealing with heavily indebted countries, for the political response to a bill collector differs greatly from that which greets a provider of finance. Such a stance by the IFIs in the context of international debt negotiations would require support from at least some of the dominant powers within each organization. Recent cases such as that of Costa Rica suggest that the required distancing may have begun.

A working dialogue must also take into account the political position of its interlocutors in the developing countries. Intensified discussions, deepened by the exchange of personnel that has been key in a number of adjustment episodes, create a possibility for the establishment of tacit coalitions between external-organization and governmental representatives in framing adjustment programs. Such coalitions between IFIs and national technocrats, often based in the ministry of finance or the central bank are a common phenomenon in IMF and World Bank relations with developing countries. Cases of successful initiation or implementation of Fund- or Bank-backed programs in the absence of support by one or more significant domestic actors are rare. Although such alliances are appealing to the IFIs and other external actors, an examination of the politics of adjustment indicates that strategies based on transnational coalitions of technocrats may be shaky. As Stephan Haggard has described, in the case of the Philippines, external agencies overestimated the influence of their technocratic allies: Marcos had shielded certain politically sensitive sectors from the technocrats' direct control. In Zambia, where abrupt failure of the negotiated program took the IFIs somewhat by surprise, they had relied not only on a small group of civil servants but also on the support of the country's leader, Kenneth Kaunda. They neglected, however, to consider the domestic political game that surrounded Kaunda—ignoring the constraints on an apparently all-powerful national leader.

These and other instances argue for widening the dialogue beyond a small technocratic core. Critics of the present patterns point to the need for pushing dialogue up to the political leadership—including those who are opposed to policy change—and down, closer to the working level.[29] Too often, dialogue has resembled proselytization of the already converted. The question of whether the dialogue should be expanded outside the government to include groups in civil society is a more difficult one. In Jamaica under Michael Manley, the Fund did engage in such discussions at the request of the government. Casting so wide a net, however, increases the risk of the IMF or the World Bank undermining its efforts to demonstrate government ownership of the program. Widening the dialogue within the government may increase consensus and commitment to policy change; outside the government, such dialogue could be manipulated by the government to lower perceptions of its responsibility for forming a program of economic policy change supported by external actors.

Any domestic political anchor for the IFIs is likely to be narrow and tentative, and cases of a unified political leadership backing a wider program of economic policy change are relatively rare. The typical narrowness of support for such sweeping programs offers fuel for critics of a conditionality of long lists, particularly in World Bank structural adjustment loans (SALs). A short list of important policy changes has major strengths a a model of conditionality, given the politics of adjustment. Since the number of domestic allies may be small, streamlined conditionality of this sort better matches their limited monitoring capabilities, particularly over other government agencies. If conditionality is very wide-ranging, it may also elicit opposition from implementing agencies that were not involved in the core dialogue that produced the program. Of course, if dialogue is widened and successful, it may well create additional allies. It would be naive, however, not to expect opposition within the state apparatus.

Increasing the public visibility of the policy dialogue might foster the conditions necessary for more effective program implementation, although great openness also entails political risks. Jeffrey Sachs and others have argued that the secrecy of such discussions and their exclusion of any but a small core from within the executive branch are a principal reason for heightened political resistance to adjustment programs. More frequent and politically visible policy discussions that are not connected to immediate decisions on borrowing would have a number of positive effects. In the case of the IMF, assigning greater importance and publicity to Article IV consultations would serve to reduce the worrying division between industrialized and developing countries. Not one of the former has turned to the Fund for use of its resources in over a decade.

When programs are negotiated in the context of policy dialogue, their implementation is likely to be improved for several reasons. As noted earlier, ongoing discussions lengthen the shadow of the future: The realization that the government will confront the Fund or the Bank in the context of such discussions at regular intervals heightens the probability of cooperation. As Paul Mosley has observed, defection from an agreed program is more likely if future relations with the external lender are sharply discounted.[30] If regular discussions making up a policy dialogue could be elevated in importance, some of the political spotlight and symbolism would also be removed from negotiations surrounding lending. Such an elevation would, however, probably mean greater publicity for the outcomes of these discussions, with the Bank and the Fund taking a clear view on the course of national economic policy. That would bring its own costs as governments might be less frank in discussing their policy dilemmas and the future course of policy if domestic political opponents could seize on the evaluation of external agencies for their own purposes.

Creating a genuine policy dialogue over time and reducing the prominence of decisions to "go to the Fund (or the Bank)" for financial support would also undercut one of the major political roles that external agencies have assumed over the years—that of "lightning rod" for domestic political opposition. The role can be seen as part of the process of coalition formation; one final means whereby a reluctant political leadership can be swung behind an adjustment program is by offering the IMF or the World Bank as a scapegoat for the painful aspects of the program. In the past, the IMF in particular tacitly accepted this role as a way to seal approval of programs. More recently, the IFIs have wisely appeared less willing to countenance this dynamic. Whatever the short-term gains in winning approval for a program by a reluctant government, external agencies that serve as lightning rods also seriously undermine claims to government ownership of a program. A recent example was a release by IMF Managing Director Michel Camdessus of letters exchanged with the Venezuelan President Perez, following riots in that country. The exchange implicitly rejected IMF responsibility for the political reaction to policies of the government's own design.[31] If an expanded policy dialogue worked, the incentives to use the IFIs as lighting rods would decline, the coercive element in the construction of programs would diminish, and government commitment would increase.

Countries whose administrative and technical capabilities make symmetrical dialogue impossible pose particular challenges for intensifying and widening policy discussions. The dilemmas for the IMF and the Bank in these cases are severe. Detailed and intrusive intervention in the administration of programs may be required if programs are to succeed, yet such intervention sets up nationalist reactions that may impede implementation in the long run. The re-expatriatization of African programs is a prominent example. Even in these cases, however, political obstacles can be reduced through the careful design of external involvement. The objectivity of analysis that supports programs can be confirmed in the eyes of national skeptics by using independent experts, a method already employed by the World Bank in certain instances.[32] The intensification of technical assistance programs could also be linked to the dialogue process to accelerate the emergence of technically trained dialogue participants.

Finance and the Politics of Adjustment with Growth

In the bargaining model of conditionality, finance is central to the power of IFIs and other lenders; it represents a major inducement for governments to surmount the political risks of an adjustment program. Future need for finance is a major deterrent, in this view, to defection from the policy conditions of an IFI-sponsored program. Even in a more harmonious model of policy dialogue, finance can serve to cement transnational coalitions by providing help to allies in their internal bargaining, permitting the supporters of a program to alter the payoffs in the domestic bargaining game.

In attempting to highlight the role of *levels* of finance on program "success" (measured in balance-of-payments equilibrium, economic growth, or political survival), conventional wisdom points in opposing directions. One view, derived from the bargaining model, argues that high levels of external finance create a temptation or *deviation effect:* With balance-of-payments pressure removed, governments can avoid the policy changes necessary for adjustment—whether the source of financial relief is foreign aid, a commodity boom, commercial bank lending, or a generous IMF or World Bank program. An alternative view points to a *reinforcement effect:* High levels of external finance increase the probability of program success, both by generating political support through economic growth and by serving as compensation for the losers in economic policy change.

Case studies of adjustment experience demonstrate both deviation and reinforcement effects, but one key conclusion that can be drawn is that neither high conditionality imposed from the outside nor generous levels of financial support alone are likely to produce adjustment with growth. One outcome in the 1980s is the *negative reinforcement* predicted by those who urge higher levels of external financial support: In many cases low financial support produced economic stagnation that undermined confidence in governments and their economic programs and resulted in limited (or no) adjustment. These cases seem to demonstrate that employing high conditionality programs to test political commitment may be of limited usefulness, unless these programs are followed by a mobilization of financial support.

On the other hand, cases of generous financial support that have also produced limited economic change, while more common in the 1970s than in the 1980s, can also be found. Neither the tightness of conditionality (and the intensiveness of external involvement in implementation) nor the level of external finance can by itself account for variation in records of reform. The conclusion drawn by Joan Nelson from a range of cases is that:

[the] level of financial support, measured either as concessional aid or as net capital flows (relative to the size of the recipients' economies or populations), bears no consistent relationship to extent of implementation of reforms. Financing for governments that pursued broad reforms varied from large to modest (or negative, in terms of net capital flows for some cases). And some countries that got very heavy financial support, like Costa Rica, made only modest progress on structural reforms.[33]

Perhaps the most interesting cases are those that have embodied the new goal of the IFIs: adjustment *with growth*. Across time, these cases consistently exhibit two characteristics. First, internal political commitment to a broad program of economic policy changes is firm; external conditionality (which often appears tight) is not very significant in arriving at the initial decision to undertake the program. Second and equally important, the generosity of financial support in these cases has been striking, with the IFIs delivering on their own promises of support and successfully catalyzing other capital flows or debt restructuring.

Indonesia in the late 1960s remains one of the prime examples of this pattern. The country had a coherent government ready to break with past patterns of economic policy, little disagreement on diagnosis of the short-term problem, and large amounts of external finance mobilized by the IFIs.[34] In the 1980s, Turkey offers a second example. Some have argued that the level of finance provided makes Turkey an exceptional case—that "these massive capital inflows virtually ensured the success of the adjustment effort."[35] Equally important, however, was the commitment made by the Turkish government to their economic program in 1980—*before* substantial outside involvement or bargaining with external agencies. In Africa, Ghana, which has undertaken a sweeping and orthodox program, was the third largest recipient of World Bank IDA funds in 1987 (after India and China); its concessional aid per capita in 1988 was twice the average for the rest of Africa.[36] Nevertheless, the IFIs did not spring immediately to support the Ghanaian program; the Jerry Rawlings government launched its program in 1983 with relatively low levels of support before external sources of finance were willing to endorse its political commitment. Despite Ghana's relatively unique position in Africa, its case does highlight the very fine balance between commitment and external support. If a coherent program is allowed to deal with economic stagnation and political backlash without adequate support from the outside, it is likely to fail (Zambia is a case in point); on the other hand, financial support alone is unlikely to stimulate the desired changes. Reading the political commitment of a government—or its ownership of a program—is crucial. A revival of genuine dialogue on the part of the IFIs, as outlined earlier, would provide far greater information for external agencies to use to gauge that support.

Commitment is also likely to increase if the IFIs are more willing to experiment by offering support to coherent programs that may deviate from orthodox prescriptions. Among the cases of heterodox shock programs, Israel provides another example of the importance of finance. Its program was the most successful of those attempted, in part because of the generous increase in U.S. assistance that supported the program.[37]

The line dividing generous and inadequate financial support from external sources is difficult to draw, but certainly the imposition of tight conditionality with limited financial support was a common pattern of failed programs during the 1980s. Overall, the country cases examined suggest that finance was at least as important as externally imposed conditionality for adjustment outcomes, and that internal political commitment to an economic program—commitment substantially shaped by the politics of adjustment—dominated both conditionality and finance.

Conclusion: Reading Politics from the Outside

If the politics of adjustment is key in the success of external advice and intervention, should outside agencies develop greater capabilities in reading domestic politics? Statements by the staff of the IMF and the World Bank suggest a keen awareness of the importance of political factors in the success or failure of stabilization programs. Indeed, external agencies have developed a number of devices, such as the use of prior actions as a test of governmental commitment for making such judgments. Nevertheless, political analysis and estimation remain implicit.

Keeping such analysis implicit is wise on the grounds of both prudence and capability. Member states might regard more explicit analysis as an unwarranted intrusion into their domestic affairs, creating even greater nationalist resistance to involvement with external agencies. The IMF and the World Bank have amassed considerable economic expertise; refined political analysis would require a costly investment in additional staff and data collection. Even more important than these considerations, however, is the manner in which explicit political analysis would complicate relations with borrowing countries. If the IFIs employed political analysis overtly, would debtor countries be more free to use political arguments in rejecting particular elements of conditionality? Issues of moral hazard would become pressing, given the even wider asymmetry of information between external agencies and national governments on political judgments: If a government argued that a particular measure would produce a political outcome fatal to the program, could an external agency judge that claim—especially when the government's own actions could produce the predicted outcome?

These cautions meet one powerful response: External agencies already are necessarily engaged in political analysis of an ad hoc variety. More modest measures than the creation of political risk analysis departments (which ill served private creditors in the 1970s and 1980s), could improve the quality of analysis that will almost certainly remain implicit. Policy dialogue itself offers a major means for reading the politics of economic policymaking in particular governments. In addition, the IFIs could do a better job of collating and making available to their own staffs the "lessons" of particular programs on the political as well as the economic front. Even such relatively small changes might require a substantial shift in self-image, as well as some costs, since there is value for external agencies in standing behind an apolitical and technocratic veil. That veil has already become tattered, however, and future relations between the IFIs and the developing countries will probably require recognition that better political analysis need not mean politicization.

Notes

[1] The literature on conditionality is vast. A particularly useful brief review of Fund practice is Andrew Crockett, "Issues in the Use of Fund Resources," *Finance & Development*, Vol. 19, No. 2 (June 1982), pp. 10–15; for recent restatements, see Constantine Michalopoulos, "World Bank Programs for Adjustment and Growth," and Manuel Guitian, "Adjustment and Economic Growth: Their Fundamental Complementarity," in Vittorio Corbo, et al., *Growth-Oriented Adjustment Programs* (Washington, D.C.: International Monetary Fund/World Bank, 1987), pp. 15–94.

[2] Barend A. de Vries, *Remaking the World Bank* (Washington, D.C.: Seven Locks Press, 1987), pp. 64, 66.

[3] Paul Mosley, *Conditionality as Bargaining Process: Structural Adjustment Lending, 1980–1986* (Princeton, N.J.: International Finance Section, Princeton University, 1987), pp. 9–18.

[4] Robert Putnam has developed the metaphor of the two-level game in "Diplomacy and Domestic Politics: The Logic of Two-Level Games," *International Organization*, Vol. 42, No. 3 (Summer 1988), pp. 427–60.

[5] Richard N. Cooper, "A Panel Discussion," in John Williamson, ed., *IMF Conditionality* (Washington, D.C.: Institute for International Economics, 1983), p. 571.

[6] For a more systematic treatment of political institutions and economic interests in the politics of adjustment, see Stephan Haggard and Robert Kaufman, "The Politics of Stabilization and Adjustment," in Jeffrey D. Sachs, ed., *Developing Country Debt and Economic Performance* (Chicago, Ill.: University of Chicago Press, 1989), pp. 209–54.

[7] For criticisms of the vagueness of posited connections between conditional lending and policy reforms, see Elliot Berg and Alan Batchelder, *Structural Adjustment Lending: A Critical View*, World Bank CPD Discussion Paper (January 1985), pp. 23–32.

[8] Ibid., p. 36.

[9] Mosley, *Conditionality as a Bargaining Process*, op. cit., p. 2.

[10] Williamson, ed., *IMF Conditionality*, op. cit., p. 131.

[11] Morris Goldstein and Peter Montiel, "Evaluating Fund Stabilization Programs with Multicountry Data: Some Methodological Pitfalls," *IMF Staff Papers*, Vol. 33, No. 2 (June 1986), p. 310.

[12] For a full elaboration of this strategy of investigation, see John Williamson, "On

Judging the Success of IMF Policy Advice," in Williamson, ed., *IMF Conditionality,* op. cit., pp. 129–43.

[13] Tony Killick, Graham Bird, Jennifer Sharpley and Mary Sutton, *The Quest for Economic Stabilisation: The IMF and the Third World,* Vol. 1 (London and New York: Heinemann Educational Books and St. Martin's Press, in association with the Overseas Development Institute, 1984), pp. 251–55, 260–61. Killick goes on to question the association of observance of performance criteria with overall implementation of programs, and observance of performance criteria with improvement in economic indicators (such as the balance of payments).

[14] Stephan Haggard, "The Politics of Adjustment: Lessons from the IMF's Extended Fund Facility," in Miles Kahler, ed., *The Politics of International Debt* (Ithaca, N.Y.: Cornell University Press, 1986), p. 158.

[15] Justin B. Zulu and Saleh M. Nsouli, *Adjustment Programs in Africa: The Recent Experience* (Washington, D.C.: International Monetary Fund, 1985), p. 13. It is worth noting that the period examined by Zulu and Nsouli was one of very loose conditionality compared to the pattern after 1981.

[16] World Bank, *Report on Adjustment Lending* (Washington, D.C., 1988), p. 89.

[17] Joan Nelson, ed., *Economic Crisis and Policy Choice: The Politics of Adjustment in the Third World* (Princeton, N.J.: Princeton University Press, forthcoming 1990). This collaborative effort covers the experience of thirteen developing countries (nineteen governments).

[18] See ibid.—a summary is provided by Joan Nelson in "Introduction: The Politics of Adjustment in the Third World," and the Ghana case is discussed by Thomas Callaghy in "Lost Between State and Market" in this forthcoming volume.

[19] Stephan Haggard, "The Political Economy of the Philippine Debt," in Nelson, ed., *Economic Crisis and Policy Choice,* op. cit.

[20] Cited in Callaghy, "Lost Between State and Market," in ibid.

[21] Haggard, "The Political Economy of the Philippine Debt," op. cit.

[22] Karen Remmer, "The Politics of Economic Stabilization: IMF Standby Programs in Latin America," 1954–1984, *Comparative Politics,* Vol. 26, No. 1 (October 1986), p. 21.

[23] Gerald K. Helleiner, "Introduction," in Helleiner, ed., *Africa and the International Monetary Fund* (Washington, D.C.: IMF, 1986), p. 8.

[24] Berg and Batchelder, *Structural Adjustment Lending,* op. cit., p. 45.

[25] Gerald K. Helleiner, "Policy-Based Program Lending: A Look at the Bank's New Role," in Richard E. Feinberg and contributors, *Between Two Worlds: The World Bank's Next Decade* (New Brunswick, N.J.: Transaction Books in cooperation with the Overseas Development Council, 1986), p. 65.

[26] "Korea's Fruitful Cooperation with the Fund," *Finance & Development,* Vol. 26, No. 1 (March 1989), p. 19.

[27] Carlos F. Díaz-Alejandro, "Comments, Chapters 11–14," in Williamson, ed., *IMF Conditionality,* op. cit., p. 345.

[28] On the CCFF, see Roger Pownall and Brian Stuart, "The IMF's Compensatory and Contingency Financing Facility," in *Finance & Development,* Vol. 25, No. 4 (December 1988), pp. 9–11.

[29] Berg and Batchelder, *Structural Adjustment Lending,* op. cit., pp. 45–46.

[30] Mosley, *Conditionality as Bargaining Process,* op. cit., p. 15.

[31] *New York Times,* 9 March 1989, p. C4.

[32] Gerald K. Helleiner, "Policy-Based Program Lending," op. cit., p. 61.

[33] Nelson, "Conclusion," in Nelson, ed., *Economic Crisis and Policy Choice,* op. cit.

[34] Mary Sutton, "Indonesia, 1966–70," in Tony Killick, Graham Bird, Jennifer Sharpley, and Mary Sutton, *The IMF and Stabilisation: Developing Country Experiences,* Vol. 2 (London: Heinemann, 1984), p. 111.

[35] Ahmed Abdallah, "Discussion," in Corbo et al., *Growth-Oriented Adjustment Programs,* op. cit., p. 142.

[36] *New York Times,* 3 January 1989, p. A4.

[37] Mario I. Blejer and Nissan Liviatan, "Fighting Hyperinflation: Stabilization Strategies in Argentina and Israel, 1985–86," *IMF Staff Papers,* Vol. 34, No. 3 (September 1987), pp. 434–35.

About the Overseas Development Council

The Overseas Development Council is a private, non-profit organization established in 1969 for the purpose of increasing American understanding of the economic and social problems confronting the developing countries and of how their development progress is related to U.S. interests. Toward this end, the Council functions as a center for policy research and analysis, a forum for the exchange of ideas, and a resource for public education. The Council's current program of work encompasses four major issue areas: trade and industrial policy, international finance and investment, development strategies and development cooperation, and U.S. foreign policy and the developing countries. ODC's work is used by policy makers in the Executive Branch and the Congress, journalists, and those concerned about U.S.-Third World relations in corporate and bank management, international and non-governmental organizations, universities, and educational and action groups focusing on specific development issues. ODC's program is funded by foundations, corporations, and private individuals; its policies are determined by a governing Board and Council. In selecting issues and shaping its work program, ODC is also assisted by a standing Program Advisory Committee.

Victor H. Palmieri is Chairman of the ODC, and Wayne Fredericks is Vice Chairman. The Council's President is John W. Sewell.

Overseas Development Council
1717 Massachusetts Ave., N.W.
Washington, D.C. 20036
Tel. (202) 234-8701

The Editors

Fragile Coalitions: The Politics of Economic Adjustment is the twelfth volume in the Overseas Development Council's series of policy books, U.S.–Third World Policy Perspectives. The co-editors of this series—often collaborating with guest editors contributing to the series —are Richard E. Feinberg and Valeriana Kallab.

Joan M. Nelson, guest editor of this volume, is a Senior Associate at the Overseas Development Council. Before joining the Council as a Visiting Fellow in 1982, she taught at the Massachussetts Institute of Technology, the Johns Hopkins University School of Advanced International Studies, and Princeton University's Woodrow Wilson School of Public and International Affairs. Dr. Nelson has been a consultant for the World Bank, the Agency for International Development, and for the International Monetary Fund, as well as a staff member of USAID. She has published books and articles on development assistance and policy dialogue, political participation, migration, and urban politics in developing nations, and the politics of economic stabilization and reform.

Since mid-1986, Dr. Nelson has co-ordinated a collegial research project on the politics of economic stabilization and structural change, funded by the Ford and Rockefeller Foundations. This volume of *Policy Perspectives* includes several papers based on partial returns from the second phase of that research project, which focuses on issues cutting across countries and regions. Other participants in the project include Thomas M. Callaghy, Stephan Haggard, Miles Kahler, Robert R. Kaufman (all represented in this volume), and Barbara Stallings. The first phase of the project focused primarily on sets of country studies, published in Joan M. Nelson, ed., *Economic Crisis and Policy Choice: The Politics of Adjustment in the Third World* (Princeton University Press, forthcoming, 1990).

Valeriana Kallab is Vice President and Director of Publications of the Overseas Development Council and co-editor of the ODC's U.S.–Third World Policy Perspectives series. She has been responsible for ODC's published output since 1972. Before joining ODC, she was a research editor and writer on international economic issues at the Carnegie Endowment for International Peace in New York. She was co-editor (with John P. Lewis) of *Development Strategies Reconsidered* and *U.S. Foreign Policy and the Third World: Agenda 1983;* and (with Guy F. Erb) of *Beyond Dependency: The Third World Speaks Out.*

Richard E. Feinberg is Executive Vice President and Director of Studies at the Overseas Development Council. Before joining ODC in 1981, he served as the Latin American specialist on the Policy Planning Staff of the U.S. Department of State, and as an international economist in the Treasury Department and with the House Banking Committee; he is also co-editor of the Policy Perspectives series. He is an adjunct professor of international finance at the Georgetown University School of Foreign Service. He has written numerous articles and books on U.S. foreign policy, Latin American politics, and international economics, including *The Intemperate Zone: The Third World Challenge to U.S. Foreign Policy* (W.W. Norton); (as editor) *Central America: International Dimensions of the Crisis*; and *Subsidizing Success: The Export-Import Bank in the U.S. Economy.*

Contributing Authors

John Waterbury is Professor of Politics and International Affairs at the Woodrow Wilson School of Public and International Affairs, Princeton University. A specialist in the political economy of the contemporary Middle East, he is author of *The Egypt of Nasser and Sadat* and co-author (with Alan Richards) of *The Political Economy of the Middle East*. He is currently at work on a comparative study of public enterprise in Egypt, India, Turkey, and Mexico.

Stephan Haggard is Associate Professor of Government and Faculty Associate of the Center for International Affairs, Harvard University. His research interests include the politics of growth and adjustment in the newly industrializing countries and American foreign economic policy. He is the co-author (with Tun-jen Cheng) of *Newly Industrializing Asia in Transition: Policy Reform and American Response* (1987); *Pathways from the Periphery: The Politics of Growth in the Newly Industrializing Countries* (forthcoming); and co-editor (with Chung-in Moon) of *Pacific Dynamics: The International Politics of Industrial Change* (1989). His articles have appeared in *World Politics, International Organization, The Annals of the American Academy of Political and Social Science, Pacific Focus, The Bulletin of Concerned Asian Scholars, Latin American Research Review,* and a number of edited collections. He will be on leave from Harvard at the World Bank in 1990 under an International Affairs Fellowship from the Council on Foreign Relations.

Robert R. Kaufman has been a Professor of Political Science at Rutgers University since 1968. A specialist in Latin America, he has written extensively on the political economy of authoritarianism in Argentina, Brazil, Chile, and Mexico, and on the politics of stabilization and adjustment. His publications include *The Politics of Debt in Argentina, Brazil and Mexico* and *Debt and Democracy in Latin America* (co-edited with Barbara Stallings). He has been a Research Fellow at the Harvard Center for International Affairs; a member of the Institute for Advanced Studies, Princeton; and a Visiting Professor at Yale. In addition to his appointment at Rutgers, he is currently affiliated as an adjunct Professor with the Columbia University Institute for Latin American and Iberian Studies.

Laurence Whitehead is an Official Fellow in Politics at Nuffield College, Oxford, and an editor of the *Journal of Latin American Studies*. He has also served as a Senior Scholar at the Latin American Program of the Woodrow Wilson International Center for Scholars in Washington, D.C., and as Acting Director of the Center for U.S.–Mexican Studies at the University of California, San Diego. His recent publications include *Transitions from Authoritarian Rule* (1986), which he co-edited with Guillermo O'Donnell and Philippe Schmitter, and *Latin American Debt and the Adjustment Crisis* (1986), co-edited with Rosemary Thorp. His current research concerns international support for the Latin American democracies, and the development of state organization in Latin America.

Thomas M. Callaghy is Associate Professor of Political Science at the University of Pennsylvania. He has also taught at Pennsylvania State and Columbia Universities. Dr. Callaghy's long-term research interests focus on the formation of states and the development of capitalism, but his most recent work has centered on contemporary political economy issues—particularly the politics of debt, structural adjustment, and privatizaton. He is a member of the above-mentioned project on the politics of economic reform in the Third World funded by the Ford and Rockefeller Foundations and directed by Joan M. Nelson. His contribution to the first product of this joint study is a chapter entitled "Lost Between State and Market: The Politics of Economic Adjustment in Ghana, Zambia, and Nigeria," to be published in Joan M. Nelson, ed., *Economic Crisis and Policy Choice: Politics of Economic Adjustment in the Third World* (Princeton University Press, forthcoming, 1990). Along with Professor John Ravenhill, Dr. Callaghy is also editing a volume on Africa's current political economy entitled *Hemmed In: Responses to Africa's Economic Dilemma,* which will appear in 1990. He is also the author of *The State-Society Struggle: Zaire in Comparative Perspective* (1984); editor of *South Africa in Southern Africa* (1983); co-editor of *Socialism in Sub-Saharan Africa: A New Assessment* (1979), and has contributed to numerous journals and edited volumes.

Miles Kahler is Professor at the Graduate School of International Relations and Pacific Studies, University of California, San Diego. Before his appointment to the faculty of the University of California in 1986, he taught at the Woodrow Wilson School of Public and International Affairs, Princeton University, and at Yale University. His recent publications include *The Politics of International Debt* (editor); *Decolonization in Britain and France: The Domestic Consequences of International Relations;* and numerous articles on comparative politics and international political economy. Professor Kahler is chair of the Committee on Foreign Policy Studies of the Social Science Research Council. He has been awarded fellowships by the Rockefeller Foundation and the National Science Foundation, and was a Council on Foreign Relations fellow at the International Monetary Fund in 1983–84.

THE FUTURE OF THE INTERNATIONAL MONETARY FUND

Catherine Gwin, Richard E. Feinberg, and contributors

The global economic environment in which we now live is radically different from the one foreseen when the International Monetary Fund was created in the wake of World War II. The important changes have to do not only with the end of U.S. economic hegemony and the demise of the fixed exchange rate system, but also with the internationalization of financial markets, shifting patterns of global production and trade, and a prolonged slowdown in global economic growth.

The Fund has not kept pace with the changes and has not been fulfilling its needed role. This volume poses the fundamental questions regarding the responsiveness of Fund policies and practices to change, and the member countries' willingness to let the Fund play a more constructive role in coping with the new realities of international monetary and financial matters. It also addresses the overarching question of the Fund's dual role—its systemic role and its role as a financial institution for countries that do not have market access, or whose access is temporarily interrupted. The study sets out a plan for revisions that must be made in light of the major changes in the global economy.

Contents:

Catherine Gwin has been a consultant to The Ford Foundation, Rockefeller Foundation, and Asia Society. She also served as a consultant for the Group of Twenty-Four's 1987 report on the future of the International Monetary Fund. From 1981-83, she was a Senior Associate at the Carnegie Endowment for International Peace, where she directed a Study Group on international financial cooperation and the management of developing-country debt. From 1980-81, she was North-South issues coordinator at the U.S. International Development Cooperation Agency. From 1976 to 1978, she was on the staff of the 1980s Project of the Council on Foreign Relations; in 1978-79, she was Staff Director of the project. Dr. Gwin has taught at the School of International Affairs of Columbia University and she has published widely in the field of development economics.

Richard E. Feinberg is vice president of the Overseas Development Council. He served as the Latin American specialist on the Policy Planning Staff of the Department of State from 1977 to 1979. He has worked as an international economist in the Treasury Department and with the House Banking Committee, and has been an adjunct professor of international finance at the Georgetown University School of Foreign Service. Dr. Feinberg has written numerous articles and books on U.S. foreign policy, Latin American politics, and international economics, including *The Intemperate Zone: The Third World Challenge to U.S. Foreign Policy* (W. W. Norton); (as editor) *Central America: International Dimensions of the Crisis* (Holmes and Meier); and *Subsidizing Success: The Export-Import Bank in the U.S. Economy* (Cambridge University Press).

U.S.-Third World Policy Perspectives, No. 13 $24.95 (cloth)
September 1989, 256 pp. $15.95 (paper)

BETWEEN TWO WORLDS:
THE WORLD BANK'S NEXT DECADE
Richard E. Feinberg and contributors

"essential reading for anybody interested in the Bank"
—The Economist

**"well-researched analysis of some of the problems con-
fronting the World Bank in the 1980s"**
—The Journal of Development Studies

In the midst of the global debt and adjustment crises, the World Bank
has been challenged to become the leading agency in North-South
fiwhich must be comprehensively addressed by the Bank's new
presinance and development. The many dimensions of this challenge
are the subject of this important volume.

As mediator between international capital markets and developing
countries, the World Bank will be searching for ways to renew the
flow of private credit and investment to Latin America and Africa.
And as the world's premier development agency, the Bank can help
formulate growth strategies appropriate to the 1990s.

The Bank's ability to design and implement a comprehensive response to these global needs is threatened by competing objectives
and uncertain priorities. Can the Bank design programs attractive to
private investors that also serve the very poor? Can it emphasize efficiency while transferring technologies that maximize labor absorp-
tion? Can it more aggressively condition loans on policy reforms without attracting the criticism that has accompanied IMF programs?

The contributors to this volume assess the role that the World Bank
can play in the period ahead. They argue for new financial and policy
initiatives and for new conceptual approaches to development, as well
as for a restructuring of the Bank, as it takes on new, systemic responsibilities in the next decade.

Contents:
Richard E. Feinberg—Overview: An Open Letter to the World Bank's Next President
Gerald K. Helleiner—Policy-Based Program Leading: A Look at the Bank's New Role
Joan M. Nelson—The Diplomacy of Policy-Based Lending
Sheldon Annis—The Shifting Grounds of Poverty Lending at The World Bank
Howard Pack—The Technological Impact of World Bank Operations
John F. H. Purcell and Michelle B. Miller—The World Bank and Private Capital
Charles R. Blitzer—Financing the World Bank

Richard E. Feinberg is vice president of the Overseas Development Council and co-
editor of the U.S.-Third World Policy Perspectives series. From 1977 to 1979, Feinberg
was Latin American specialist on the policy planning staff of the U.S. Department of
State. He has also served as an international economist in the U.S. Treasury Department and with the House Banking Committee. He is currently also adjunct professor of
international finance at the Georgetown University School of Foreign Service. Feinberg is the author of numerous books as well as journal and newspaper articles on U.S.
foreign policy, Latin American politics, and international economics.

U.S.-Third World Policy Perspectives, No. 7 ISBN: 0-88738-123-5 (cloth) $19.95
June 1986, 208 pp. ISBN: 0-88738-665-2 (paper) $12.95

U.S. FOREIGN POLICY AND ECONOMIC REFORM IN THREE GIANTS: THE USSR, CHINA, AND INDIA

Richard E. Feinberg, John Echeverri-Gent, Friedemann Müller, and contributors

Three of the largest and strategically most important nations in the world—the Soviet Union, China, and India—are currently in the throes of historic change. The reforms in the giants are transforming global economic and geopolitical relations. The United States must reexamine central tenets of its foreign policy if it is to seize the opportunities presented by these changes.

This pathbreaking study analyzes economic reform in the giants and its implications for U.S. foreign policy. It assesses the impact of the reforms on the livelihood of the nearly half the world's population living in their societies. Each of the giants is opening up its economy to foreign trade and investment. What consequences will this new outward orientation have for international trade, and how should U.S. policy respond to these developments? Each giant is attempting to catch up to global technological frontiers by absorbing foreign technologies; in what areas might cooperation enhance American interests, and in what areas must the U.S. protect its competitive and strategic assets? What role can key international economic institutions like the GATT, the IMF, and the World Bank play to help integrate the giants into the international economy?

Economic reform in the giants has important consequences for their political systems. What measures can and should the United States take to encourage political liberalization? How will the reforms affect the foreign policies of the giants, and what impact will this have on U.S. geopolitical interests?

The contributors suggest how U.S. foreign policy should anticipate these new circumstances in ways that enhance international cooperation and security.

Richard E. Feinberg, John Echeverri-Gent, and Friedemann Müller—Overview: Economic Reform in the Giants and U.S. Policy

Friedemann Müller—Economic Reform in the USSR

Rensselaer W. Lee III—Economic Reform in China

John Echeverri-Gent—Economic Reform in India

John Echeverri-Gent, Friedemann Müller, and Rensselaer W. Lee III—The Politics of Economic Reform in the Giants

Thomas Naylor—Economic Reforms and International Trade

Richard P. Suttmeier—Technology Transfer to the Giants: Opportunities and Challenges

Elena Borisovna Arefieva—The Geopolitical Consequences of Reform in the Giants

---

Richard E. Feinberg is vice president of the Overseas Development Council and co-editor of the U.S.-Third World Policy Perspectives series. From 1977 to 1979, Feinberg was Latin American specialist on the policy planning staff of the U.S. Department of State.

John Echeverri-Gent is a visiting fellow at the Overseas Development Council and an assistant professor at the University of Virginia. His publications are in the fields of comparative public policy and the political economy of development in India.

Friedemann Müller is a visiting fellow at the Overseas Development Council and a senior research associate at Stiftung Wissenschaft und Politik, Ebenhausen, West Germany. His publications on the Soviet and Eastern European economies have focused on economic reform, energy policy, and East-West trade.

U.S.-Third World Policy Perspectives, No. 14
Winter 1989, 256 pp.

$24.95 (cloth)
$15.95 (paper)

ENVIRONMENT AND THE POOR: DEVELOPMENT STRATEGIES FOR A COMMON AGENDA

H. Jeffrey Leonard and contributors

Few aspects of development are as complex and urgent as the need to reconcile anti-poverty and pro-environmental goals. Do both of these important goals—poverty alleviation and environmental sustainability—come in the same package? Or are there necessary trade-offs and must painful choices be made?

A basic premise of this volume is that environmental degradation and intractable poverty are often especially pronounced in particular ecological and social settings across the developing world. These twin crises of development and the environment can and must be addressed jointly. But they require differentiated strategies for the kinds of physical environments in which poor people live. This study explores these concerns in relation to irrigated areas, arid zones, moist tropical forests, hillside areas, urban centers, and unique ecological settings.

The overview chapter highlights recent efforts to advance land and natural resource management, and some of the real and perceived conflicts between alleviating poverty and protecting the environment in the design and implementation of development policy. The chapters that follow offer economic investment and natural resource management options for reducing poverty and maintaining ecological balance for six different areas of the developing world.

Contents:

H. Jeffrey Leonard—Overview

Montague Yudelman—Maintaining Production on Irrigated Lands

J. Dirck Stryker—Technology, Human Pressure, and Ecology in Arid Regions

John O. Browder—Agricultural Alternatives for Humid Tropical Forests

A. John De Boer—Sustainable Approaches to Hillside Agriculture

Tim E. J. Campbell—Resource Dilemmas in the Urban Environment

Alison Jolly—Meeting Human Needs in Unique Ecological Settings

H. Jeffrey Leonard, guest editor of this volume, is the vice president of the World Wildlife Fund and The Conservation Foundation and Director of the Fairfield Osborn Center for Economic Development. Dr. Leonard has been at The Foundation since 1976. He is the author of several recent books, including *Pollution and the Struggle for the World Product, Natural Resources and Economic Development in Central America,* and *Are Environmental Regulations Driving U.S. Industries Overseas?* He is also editor of *Divesting Nature's Capital: The Political Economy of Environmental Abuse in the Third World* and *Business and Environment: Toward a Common Ground.*

U.S.-Third World Policy Perspectives, No. 11
Summer 1989, 256 pp.

$24.95 (cloth)
$15.95 (paper)

STRENGTHENING THE POOR: WHAT HAVE WE LEARNED?

John P. Lewis and contributors

"bound to influence policymakers and make a major contribution to renewed efforts to reduce poverty"
—B. T. G. Chidzero, Minister of Finance,
Economic Planning, and Development,
Government of Zimbabwe

"deserves wide readership within the broader development community"
—Barber B. Conable, President,
The World Bank

The issue of poverty alleviation—of strengthening the poor—is now being brought back toward the top of the development policy agenda.

The current refocusing on poverty is not just a matter of turning back the clock. Anti-poverty initiatives for the 1990s must respond to a developing world and a policy environment that in many ways differs dramatically from that of the 1970s and even the 1980s. Much has been accomplished during and since the last thrust of anti-poverty policy. The poor themselves have in some cases become more vocal, organized, and effective in pressing their own priorities. A great deal of policy experience has accrued. And national governments, donor agencies, and non-governmental organizations now employ a much wider range of tools for poverty alleviation.

Strengthening the Poor provides a timely assessment of these changes and experience. In an overview essay, John Lewis draws important policy lessons both from poverty alleviation's period of high salience in the 1970s and from its time of lowered attention in the adjustment-accentuating 1980s. An impressive cluster of U.S. and developing-country authors react to these propositions from diverse points of view.

Contents:

U.S.-Third World Policy Perspectives, No. 10
1988, 256 pp.

ISBN: 0-88738-267-3 (cloth) $19.95
ISBN: 0-88738-768-3 (paper) $12.95

DEVELOPMENT STRATEGIES RECONSIDERED
John P. Lewis and Valeriana Kallab, editors

"First-rate, comprehensive analysis—presented
in a manner that makes it extremely valuable
to policy makers."
—Robert R. Nathan
Robert Nathan Associates

Important differences of opinion are emerging about the national strategies best suited for advancing economic growth and equity in the difficult global adjustment climate of the late 1980s.

Proponents of the "new orthodoxy"—the perspective headquartered at the World Bank and favored by the Reagan administration as well as by a number of other bilateral donor governments—are "carrying forward with redoubled vigor the liberalizing, pro-market strains of the thinking of the 1960s and 1970s. They are very mindful of the limits of government." And they are "emphatic in advocating export-oriented growth to virtually all comers."

Other prominent experts question whether a standardized prescription of export-led growth can meet the needs of big low-income countries in the latter 1980s as well as it did those of small and medium-size middle-income countries in the 1960s and 1970s. They are concerned about the special needs of low-income Africa. And they see a great deal of unfinished business under the heading of poverty and equity.

In this volume, policy syntheses are proposed to reconcile the goals of growth, equity, and adjustment; to strike fresh balances between agricultural and industrial promotion and between capital and other inputs; and to reflect the interplay of democracy and development.

Contents:

John P. Lewis—Overview —Development Promotion: A Time for Regrouping
Irma Adelman—A Poverty-Focused Approach to Development Policy
John W. Mellor—Agriculture on the Road to Industrialization
Jagdish N. Bhagwati—Rethinking Trade Strategy
Leopoldo Solis and Aurelio Montemayor—A Mexican View of the Choice Between Inward and Outward Orientation
Colin I. Bradford, Jr.—East Asian "Models": Myths and Lessons
Alex Duncan—Aid Effectiveness in Raising Adaptive Capacity in the Low-Income Countries
Atul Kohli—Democracy and Development

John P. Lewis is Professor of Economics and International Affairs at Princeton University's Woodrow Wilson School of Public and International Affairs. He is simultaneously senior advisor to the Overseas Development Council and chairman of its Program Advisory Committee. From 1979 to 1981, Dr. Lewis was chairman of the OECD's Development Assistance Committee (DAC). From 1982 to 1985, he was chairman of the three-year World Bank/IMF Task Force on Concessional Flows. He has served as a member of the U.N. Committee for Development Planning. For many years, he has alternated between academia and government posts (as Member of the Council of Economic Advisors, 1963-64, and Director of the USAID Mission to India, 1964-69), with collateral periods of association with The Brookings Institution, The Ford Foundation, and the World Bank.

Valeriana Kallab is vice president and director of publications of the Overseas Development Council and series co-editor of the ODC's U.S.-Third World Policy Perspectives series. She has been responsible for ODC's published output since 1972. Before joining ODC, she was a research editor and writer on international economic issues at the Carnegie Endowment for International Peace in New York.

U.S.-Third World Policy Perspectives, No. 5   ISBN: 0-88738-044-1 (cloth) $19.95
1986, 208 pp.   ISBN: 0-87855-991-4 (paper) $12.95

GROWTH, EXPORTS, AND JOBS IN A CHANGING WORLD ECONOMY: AGENDA 1988

John W. Sewell, Stuart K. Tucker, and contributors

"particularly timely, as the Administration and Congress face critical decisions on the trade bill, the budget, and other issues affecting the economic future of the U.S. and countries around the globe"
—Frank C. Carlucci, Secretary of Defense

Agenda 1988, the eleventh of ODC's well-known assessments of U.S. policy toward the developing countries, contributes uniquely to the ongoing debate on U.S. jobs and trade competition with other nations..

The administration that takes office in 1989 faces a situation without precedent in the post-1945 period. Like many developing countries, the United States has to balance its trade accounts, service its foreign debts, and rebuild its industrial base. The challenge is twofold.

The immediate task is to restore the international economic position of the United States by taking the lead in devising measures to support renewed *global* growth, especially rapid growth in the developing countries.

Meanwhile, however, the world is on the threshold of a Third Industrial Revolution. Rapid technological advances are radically changing the familiar economic relationships between developed and developing countries. The kinds of policies needed to adjust to these technology-driven changes— policies on education, training, research and development—generally have longer lead times than the immediate measures needed to stimulate global growth. In the next four years, the United States must therefore proceed on *both* fronts at the same time.

John W. Sewell—Overview: The Dual Challenge: Managing the Economic Crisis and Technological Change
Manuel Castells and Laura D'Andrea Tyson—High-Technology Choices Ahead: Restructuring Interdependence
Jonathan D. Aronson—The Service Industries: Growth, Trade, and Development Prospects
Robert L. Paarlberg—U.S. Agriculture and the Developing World: Opportunities for Joint Gains
Raymond F. Mikesell—The Changing Demand for Industrial Raw Materials
Ray Marshall—Jobs: The Shifting Structure of Global Employment
Stuart K. Tucker—Statistical Annexes: U.S.-Third World Interdependence, 1988

John W. Sewell has been president of the Overseas Development Council since January, 1980. From 1977 to 1979, as the Council's executive vice president, he directed ODC's programs of research and public education. Prior to joining the Council in 1971, Mr. Sewell directed the communications program of the Brookings Institution. He also served in the Foreign Service of the United States. A contributor to past *Agenda* assessments, he is co-author of *Rich Country Interests and Third World Development* and *The Ties That Bind: U.S. Interests in Third World Development*. He is a frequent author and lecturer on U.S. relations with the developing countries.

Stuart K. Tucker is a fellow at the Overseas Development Council. Prior to joining ODC in 1984, he was a research consultant for the Inter-American Development Bank. He has written on U.S. international trade policy, including the linkage between the debt crisis and U.S. exports and jobs. He also prepared the Statistical Annexes in ODC's *Agenda 1985-86*.

U.S.-Third World Policy Perspectives, No. 9
1988, 286 pp.

ISBN: 088738-196-0 (cloth) $19.95
ISBN: 0-88738-718-7 (paper) $12.95

THE UNITED STATES AND MEXICO: FACE TO FACE WITH NEW TECHNOLOGY

Cathryn L. Thorup and contributors

Rapid technological advance is fast changing economic and political relations between industrial and advanced developing countries. The new technologies encompass innovations in automation and robotization, the substitution of synthetic for natural materials, advances in communications and information technology, and changes in social organization. These advances are transforming production, trade, and investment in manufactures, commodities, and services—with major repercussions on jobs, wages, and politics in many countries.

This study explores what adjustment to this worldwide transformation means close to home—for people and policies in Mexico and the United States, and for relations between the two nations.

The authors come from both sides of the border—bringing together varied experience and expertise from government, business, and academic institutions. They highlight the interplay of economic, political, social, and cultural forces in the process of technological change. Among the themes they explore are the relationships between technological advance and employment, immigration, foreign debt, and protectionism. From their analysis of the objectives and policies of both countries emerge insights into the politics of technology change—the policy constraints faced in each country, the limits of political will, and the changing horizons of domestic interest groups.

The study draws together specific recommendations on improving the efficiency of bilateral economic interaction, reducing the adjustment costs of technological change, and avoiding diplomatic tensions between the two nations.

Contents:

Cathryn L. Thorup is the director of the U.S.-Mexico Project of the Overseas Development Council. Prior to joining ODC in 1980, she spent six years in Mexico, studying and working as a journalist for the Mexican news magazine *Razones*. She has written extensively on U.S. policymaking toward Mexico, conflict management in U.S.-Mexican relations, regional security, and Mexican economic and political reform. Ms. Thorup is a member of the Board of Directors of the Consortium for U.S. Research Programs for Mexico (PROFMEX).

U.S.-Third World Policy Perspectives, No. 8
1987, 238 pp.

ISBN: 0-88738-120-0 (cloth) $19.95
ISBN: 0-88738-663-6 (paper) $12.95

HARD BARGAINING AHEAD: U.S. TRADE POLICY AND DEVELOPING COUNTRIES

Ernest H. Preeg and contributors

> **"a well-integrated volume which analyzes major trade problems and sets forth concrete, reasonable proposals for dealing with them in GATT negotiations as well as bilaterally"**
> —*Foreign Affairs*

U.S.-Third World trade relations are at a critical juncture. Trade conflicts are exploding as subsidies, import quotas, and "voluntary" export restraints have become commonplace. The United States is struggling with record trade and budget deficits. Developing countries, faced with unprecedented debt problems, continue to restrain imports and stimulate exports.

For both national policies and future multilateral negotiations, the current state of the North-South trade relationship presents a profound dilemma. Existing problems of debt and unemployment cannot be solved without growth in world trade. While many developing countries would prefer an export-oriented development strategy, access to industrialized-country markets will be in serious doubt if adjustment policies are not implemented. Consequently, there is an urgent need for more clearly defined mutual objectives and a strengthened policy framework for trade between the industrialized and the developing countries.

In this volume, distinguished practitioners and academics identify specific policy objectives for the United States on issues that will be prominent in the new round of GATT negotiations.

Contents:

Ernest H. Preeg—Overview: An Agenda for U.S. Trade Policy Toward Developing Countries
William E. Brock—Statement: U.S. Trade Policy Toward Developing Countries
Anne O. Krueger and Constantine Michalopoulos—Developing-Country Trade Policies and the International Economic System
Henry R. Nau—The NICs in a New Trade Round
C. Michael Aho—U.S. Labor-Market Adjustment and Import Restrictions
John D. A. Cuddy—Commodity Trade
Adebayo Adedeji—Special Measures for the Least Developed and Other Low-Income Countries
Sidney Weintraub—Selective Trade Liberalization and Restriction
Stuart K. Tucker—Statistical Annexes

Ernest H. Preeg, a career foreign service officer and recent visiting fellow at the Overseas Development Council, has had long experience in trade policy and North-South economic relations. He was a member of the U.S. delegation to the GATT Kennedy Round of negotiations and later wrote a history and analysis of those negotiations, *Traders and Diplomats* (The Brookings Institution, 1969). Prior to serving as American ambassador to Haiti (1981-82), he was deputy chief of mission in Lima, Peru (1977-80), and deputy secretary of state for international finance and development (1976-77).

U.S.-Third World Policy Perspectives, No. 4   ISBN: 0-88738-043-3 (cloth) $19.95
1985, 220 pp.   ISBN: 0-87855-987-6 (paper) $12.95

INVESTING IN DEVELOPMENT:
NEW ROLES FOR PRIVATE CAPITAL?

Theodore H. Moran and contributors

"excellent and exceptionally timely book"
—Foreign Affairs

The tone of the debate about foreign direct investment in Third World development has changed dramatically since the 1970s. There are expectations in both North and South that multinational corporations can play a key role in restoring growth, replacing aid, providing capital to relieve the burden on commercial bank lending, and (together with the private sectors in the local economies) lead to an era of healthier and more balanced growth.

To what extent are these expectations justified? This volume provides a reassessment of the impact of multinational corporate operations on Third World development. It covers not only direct equity investment in natural resources and manufacturing, but non-equity arrangements extending to agriculture and other sectors as well. It examines whether the efforts of less developed countries to attract and control multinational corporations have constituted a serious "distortion" of trade that threatens jobs in the home nations. It analyzes the link between international companies and the "umbrella" of World Bank co-financing as a mechanism to reduce risk. Finally, it attempts to estimate how much of the "gap" in commercial bank lending might plausibly be filled by direct corporate investment over the next decade.

In each case, it draws policy conclusions for host governments, for home governments (focused particularly on the United States), for multilateral institutions such as the World Bank and the agencies of the United Nations, and for the multinational firms themselves.

Theodore H. Moran—Overview: The Future of Foreign Direct Investment in the Third World
Joseph M. Grieco—Foreign Direct Investment and Third World Development: Theories and Evidence
Dennis J. Encarnation and Louis T. Wells, Jr.—Evaluating Foreign Investment
Vincent Cable and Bishakha Mukherjee—Foreign Investment in Low-Income Developing Countries
David J. Glover—Multinational Corporations and Third World Agriculture
Charles P. Oman—New Forms of Investment in Developing Countries
Stephen Guisinger—Host-Country Policies to Attract and Control Foreign Investment
David J. Goldsbrough—Investment Trends and Prospects: The Link with Bank Lending

Theodore H. Moran is director of Georgetown University's Landegger Program in International Business Diplomacy as well as professor and member of the Executive Council of the Georgetown University School of Business Administration. A former member of the Policy Planning Staff of the Department of State with responsibilities including investment issues, Dr. Moran has since 1971 been a consultant to corporations, governments, and multilateral agencies on investment strategy, international negotiations, and political risk assessment. His publications include many articles and five major books on the issues explored in this new volume.

U.S.-Third World Policy Perspectives, No. 6   ISBN: 0-88738-074-3 (cloth) $19.95
1986, 208 pp.   ISBN: 0-88738-644-X (paper) $12.95

ADJUSTMENT CRISIS IN THE THIRD WORLD

Richard E. Feinberg and Valeriana Kallab, editors

**"major contribution to the literature on the
adjustment crisis"**
—B. T. G. Chidzero
Minister of Finance, Economic Planning,
and Development, Government of Zimbabwe

Just how the debt and adjustment crisis of Third World countries is handled, by them and by international agencies and banks, can make a big difference in the pace and quality of *global* recovery.

Stagnating international trade, sharp swings in the prices of key commodities, worsened terms of trade, high interest rates, and reduced access to commercial bank credits have slowed and even reversed growth in many Third World countries. Together, these trends make "adjustment" of both demand and supply a central problem confronting policymakers in most countries in the mid-1980s. Countries must bring expenditures into line with shrinking resources in the short run, but they also need to alter prices and take other longer-range steps to expand the resource base in the future—to stimulate investment, production, and employment. Already low living standards make this an especially formidable agenda in most Third World nations.

What can be done to forestall the more conflictive phase of the debt crisis that now looms ahead? How can developing countries achieve adjustment *with growth?* The contributors to this volume share the belief that more constructive change is possible and necessary.

Contents:
Richard E. Feinberg—The Adjustment Imperative and U.S. Policy
Albert Fishlow—The Debt Crisis: Round Two Ahead?
Tony Killick, Graham Bird, Jennifer Sharpley, and Mary Sutton—
The IMF: Case for a Change in Emphasis
Stanley Please—The World Bank: Lending for Structural Adjustment
Joan M. Nelson—The Politics of Stabilization
Colin I. Bradford, Jr.—The NICs: Confronting U.S. "Autonomy"
Riordan Roett—Brazil's Debt Crisis
Lance Taylor—Mexico's Adjustment in the 1980s: Look Back Before Leaping Ahead
DeLisle Worrell—Central America and the Caribbean: Adjustment in Small, Open
Economies

Richard E. Feinberg is vice president of Overseas Development Council and co-editor of the Policy Perspectives series. Before joining ODC in 1981, he served as the Latin American specialist on the Policy Planning Staff of the U.S. Department of State, and as an international economist in the Treasury Department and with the House Banking Committee. He is the author of numerous books as well as journal and newspaper articles on U.S. foreign policy, Latin American politics, and international economic and financial issues.

Valeriana Kallab is vice president and director of publications of the Overseas Development Council and series co-editor of the ODC's U.S.-Third World Policy Perspectives series. She has been responsible for ODC's published output since 1972. Before joining ODC, she was a research editor and writer on international economic issues at the Carnegie Endowment for International Peace in New York.

U.S.-Third World Policy Perspectives, No. 1   ISBN: 0-88738-040-9 (cloth) $19.95
1984, 220 pp.   ISBN: 0-87855-988-4 (paper) $12.95